Microwave
HERBS & SPICES

BRAMLEY BOOKS

Recipes Compiled, Prepared and Styled by Jacqueline Bellefontaine
Edited by Judith Ferguson
Photography by Peter Barry
Designed by Sara Cooper
Produced by David Gibbon,
   Gerald Hughes and Ted Smart
CLB 1963
This edition published 1987 by Bramley Books, Godalming, Surrey.
© 1987 Colour Library Books Ltd., Guildford, Surrey.
Printed and bound in Barcelona, Spain by Cronion, S.A.
ISBN 0-86283-573-9

Acknowledgement
The publishers wish to thank Samsung Electronics (UK) Ltd for the loan of microwave ovens, Corning Ltd for providing Pyrex and microwave cookware dishes and Lakeland Plastics of Windermere, Cumbria for the supply of cookware and accessories.
The publishers also wish to thank Peter and Jackie Petts of The Herbary Prickwillow, Ely, Cambs. CB7 4SJ (tel: 0353 88 456), suppliers by post of fresh cut herbs and container-grown herb plants, for providing herb produce and plants for use in the preparation and presentation of recipes in this book.

CONTENTS
General Introduction page 3

GENERAL INTRODUCTION

People are usually of two minds about microwave ovens. Experienced cooks are sceptical. Inexperienced cooks are mystified. Most people who don't own one think a microwave oven is an expensive luxury. Those of us who have one, though, would find it difficult to give it up. Great advances have been made in the design and capabilities of microwave ovens since the demand for them first began in the Sixties. With so many kinds of ovens available, both beginners and advanced cooks can find one that best suits their particular needs.

How Microwave Ovens Work

Microwave ovens, whatever the make or model, do have certain things in common. The energy that makes fast cooking possible is comprised of electromagnetic waves converted from electricity. Microwaves are a type of high frequency radio wave. The waves are of short length, hence the name microwave.

Inside the oven is a magnetron, which converts ordinary electricity into microwaves. A wave guide channels the microwaves into the oven cavity, and a stirrer fan circulates them evenly. Microwaves are attracted to the particles of moisture that form part of any food. As the microwaves are absorbed, to a depth of about 4-5cm/1½-2 inches, they cause the water molecules in the food to vibrate, about 2000 million times a second. This generates the heat that cooks the food. The heat reaches the centre of the food by conduction, just as in ordinary cooking. However, this is accomplished much faster than in conventional cooking because no heat is generated until the waves are absorbed by the food. All the energy is concentrated on cooking the food and not on heating the oven itself or the baking dishes. Standing time is often necessary to allow the food to continue cooking after it is removed from the oven.

Most microwave ovens have an ON indicator light and a timer control. Some timer controls look like minute timers, while others are calibrated in seconds up to 50 seconds and minutes up to 30 minutes. This can vary slightly; some models have a 10 minute interval setting. Some ovens have a separate ON-OFF switch, while others switch on with the timer or power setting. Almost all have a bell or buzzer to signal the end of cooking time.

Microwave Oven Features

At this point, things really begin to diversify. Different terms are used for the same power setting depending on what brand of oven you buy. Some ovens have a wider range of different settings as well. Chart No. 1 on power settings reconciles most of the popular terms.

Some ovens come equipped with a temperature probe which allows you to cook food according to its internal temperature instead of by time. It is most useful for roasting large cuts of meat. The probe needle is inserted into the thickest part of the food and the correct temperature set on the attached control. When that internal temperature is reached, the oven automatically turns off, or switches to a low setting to keep the food warm. Special microwave thermometers are also available to test internal temperature and can be used inside the oven. Conventional thermometers must never be used inside a microwave oven, but can be used outside.

A cooking guide is a feature on some ovens, either integrated into the control panel or on the top or side of the oven housing. It is really a summary of the information found in the instruction and recipe booklet that accompanies every oven. However, it does act as a quick reference and so can be a time saver.

CHART 1 Power Setting Comparison Chart

	Other Terms and Wattages	Uses
Low	ONE or TWO, KEEP WARM, 25%, SIMMER, DEFROST. 75-300 watts.	Keeping food warm. Softening butter, cream cheese and chocolate. Heating liquid to dissolve yeast. Gentle cooking.
Medium	THREE or FOUR, 50%, STEW, BRAISE, ROAST, REHEAT, MEDIUM-LOW, FIVE, 40%, MEDIUM-HIGH, SIX, 60-75%.. 400-500 watts.	Roasting meat and poultry. Stewing and braising less tender cuts of meat. Baking cakes and custards. Cooking hollandaise sauces.
High	SEVEN, FULL, ROAST, BAKE, NORMAL, 100%.	Quick cooking. Meats, fish, vegetables, biscuits/cookies, pasta, rice, breads, pastry, desserts.

Turntables eliminate the need for rotating baking dishes during cooking, although when using a square or loaf dish you may need to change its position from time to time anyway. Turntables are usually glass or ceramic and can be removed for easy cleaning. Of all the special features available, turntables are one of the most useful.

Certain ovens have one or more shelves so that several dishes can be accommodated at once. Microwave energy is higher at the top of the oven than on the floor and the more you cook at once the longer it all takes. However, these ovens accommodate larger baking dishes than those with turntables.

If you do a lot of entertaining, then an oven with a keep warm setting is a good choice. These ovens have a very low power setting that can keep food warm without further cooking for up to one hour. If you want to programme your oven like a computer, choose one with a memory control that can switch settings automatically during the cooking cycle.

Browning elements are now available built into microwave ovens. They look and operate much the same as conventional electric grills. If you already have a grill, you probably don't need a browning element. Some of the most recent ovens allow the browning element to be used at the same time as the microwave setting, which is a plus.

Combination ovens seem to be the answer to the problem of browning in a microwave oven. While the power settings go by different names in different models, generally there is a setting for microwave cooking alone, a convection setting with conventional electric heat and a setting which combines the two for almost the speed of microwave cooking with the browning ability of convection heat. However, the wattage is usually lower than in standard microwave ovens, and so cooking time will be slightly longer.

On combination settings, use recipes developed for microwave ovens, but follow the instructions with your particular oven for times and settings. Some ovens have various temperature settings to choose from. Breads, poultry, meat and pastries brown beautifully in these ovens, and conventional baking dishes, even metal, can be used with a special insulating mat. Beware of certain plastics though, as they can melt in a combination oven.

You can have your microwave oven built into the same unit as your conventional oven. Microwave ovens are best situated at eye level. In fact, there are now units available with gas or electric cooktops and a microwave oven underneath where the conventional oven used to be.

Safety and Cleaning

One of the questions most commonly asked is "Are microwave ovens safe to use?" They are safe because they have safety features built into them and they go through rigorous tests by their manufacturers and by independent agencies.

If you look at a number of microwave ovens you will see that the majority of them are lined with metal, and metal will not allow microwaves to pass through. The doors have special seals to keep the microwaves inside the oven and have cut-out devices to cut off microwave energy immediately the door is opened. There are no pans to upset, no open flames or hot elements and the interior of the oven stays cool enough to touch. Although microwave ovens don't heat baking dishes, the heat generated by the cooking food does, so it is a good idea to use oven gloves or pot holders to remove dishes from the oven. It is wise periodically to check the door of your oven to make sure it has not been bent. Check latches and hinges, too, to make sure they are in good working order. Don't use baking dishes that are too large to allow the turntable to rotate freely; this can cause the motor to over-heat or cause dents in the oven sides and door, lowering efficiency and affecting safety of operation.

Microwave ovens are cleaner and more hygienic to cook with than conventional gas and electric ovens. Foods do not spatter as much and spills do not burn, so clean-up is faster. The turntables and shelves can be removed for easier cleaning. Use non-abrasive cleansers and scrubbers, and be sure to wipe up

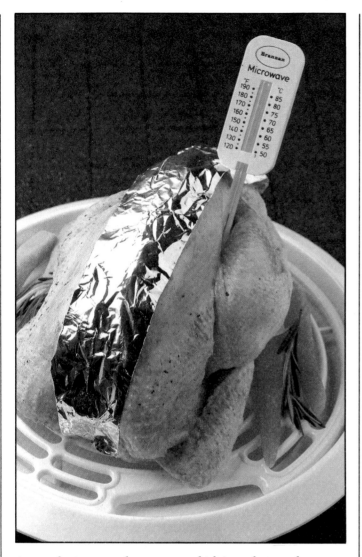

A special microwave thermometer, which·is used to test the internal temperature of the food, can be used inside the oven.

any residue so that it does not build up around the door seals. Faster cooking times and lower electricity consumption combine to make microwave ovens cheaper to run, especially for cooking small amounts of food, than conventional ovens.

Once you have chosen your oven and understand what makes it work, the fun of cooking begins. There are some basic rules to remember, however, as with conventional cooking, but most of them are common sense.

Quantity

Food quantities affect cooking times. For example, one baked potato will take about 3-4 minutes, two will take about 6-7 minutes, four will take 10-11 minutes. Generally, if you double the quantity of a recipe, you need to increase the cooking time by about half as much again.

Density and Shape

The denser the food, the longer the cooking time. A large piece of meat is bound to take longer to cook than something light and porous like a cake or a loaf of bread. When cooking foods of various densities or shapes at the same time, special arrangements are necessary. For instance, place the thicker part of the food to the outside of the dish, thinner part toward the middle. Arrange pieces of food in a circle whenever possible, and in a round dish. If neither of these arrangements is possible, cover the thinner or less dense part of the food with foil for part of the cooking time. Rearrange and turn over such foods as asparagus or broccoli spears several times during cooking if they will not fit into your round dishes without considerable trimming.

Size

The smaller a piece of food the quicker it will cook. Pieces of food of the same kind and size will cook at the same rate. Add smaller or faster-cooking foods further along in the cooking time, such as mushrooms to a stew. If you have a choice of cooking heights, put food that is larger and can take more heat above food that is smaller and more delicate.

Covering

Most foods will cook, reheat or defrost better when covered. Use special covers that come with your cookware or simple cover with cling film. This covering must be pierced to release steam, otherwise it can balloon and possibly burst. Tight covering can give meat and poultry a "steamed" taste. Greaseproof paper or paper towels can also be used to keep in the heat and increase cooking efficiency.

Sugar or Fat Content

High sugar or fat content in certain foods means they will absorb microwave energy faster and reach a higher temperature. It is wise to cover food that will spatter, such as bacon, and to protect cakes that have very sugary toppings.

Standing Time

Microwave recipes usually advise leaving food to stand for 5-10 minutes after removal from the oven. Slightly undercooking the food allows the residual heat to finish it off, and microwave recipes take this into consideration. Meat and baked potatoes are usually wrapped in foil to contain the heat. Standing time also makes meat easier to carve. Cakes, breads and pastries should be left on a flat surface for their standing time as this helps to cook their bases. In general, foods benefit from being covered during standing time.

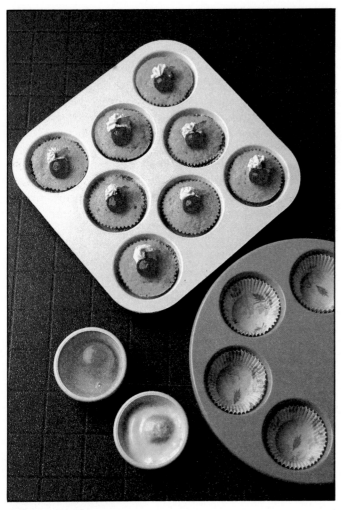

Above and left: the number and variety of different baking dishes and the range of equipment for the microwave is vast.

Equipment and Cookware

The number of different baking dishes and the range of equipment for microwave cooking is vast. There are so many highly specialised dishes for specific needs that to list them all would take up almost the whole of this book!

Explore cookware departments and find your own favourites. Follow your oven instruction booklet carefully since it will give you good advice on which cookware is best for your particular oven. Some dishes, lightweight plastics and even some hard plastics can't be used on combination settings. The temperature is too high and the dishes will melt or break. Most metal cookware can be used successfully in combination ovens, following the manufacturers guidelines. I have had less than satisfactory results with certain aluminium pans in my combination oven, so experimentation is essential. Paper bags can catch fire on High settings, and I have had the same experience with silicone-coated paper, although its use is often recommended. Microwave energy penetrates round shapes particularly efficiently, so round dishes and ring moulds work very well. The turntable can also be cooked on directly for such foods as scones or meringues or used for reheating foods like bread or coffee cakes.

For foods that are likely to boil over, like jams and soups, use the largest, deepest bowl that will fit into the oven cavity. Whole fish can be cooked in a cooking bag and curved to fit the shape of the turntable if they are too large to lie flat.

Browning dishes do work and the results are impressive. There are different designs and some have lids so that meat can be browned and finished off as a braise or stew in the same dish. Covering foods like chops or nut cutlets also speeds up the browning process. These dishes need to be preheated for between 4 to 8 minutes, depending on manufacturers instructions, and will get extremely hot. Use oven gloves or pot holders to remove browning dishes from the oven and set them on a heatproof mat to protect work surfaces. Butter will brown very fast, and steaks and chops can be seared. Stir frying is possible in a microwave oven with the use of a browning tray, and sausages brown beautifully without the shrinkage of conventional grilling or frying. These dishes can also be useful for browning a flour and fat roux for making sauces and gravies.

Cooking Poultry, Meat and Game

Moisture evaporates less readily during microwave cooking, so meat does not dry out. The fat in poultry will turn brown during cooking, but only in whole birds. Single joints of chicken or other poultry cook too quickly for the fat to brown. A thin layer of fat left on pork or beef for roasting will also brown, although it will not crisp. Fat is important to help keep the meat moist, but if you prefer to take it off, do so after cooking, or remember to baste frequently and cover the meat. There are a number of bastes, coatings and seasonings, some especially developed for microwave cooking, that can be used to give an appetizing brownness to meat and poultry.

Choose boned and rolled joints and cuts of meat that are a uniform thickness and shape. If this isn't possible, the next best thing is covering the thinner parts with foil for part of the cooking time. This trick with foil is also useful on poultry to cover the leg ends and the meat along the length of the breast bone. For poultry joints, cover the thinner ends of the breasts and the drumsticks.

Less tender cuts of meat, such as those for stewing, need to be cooked on a medium setting after initial browning. High settings can toughen these cuts of meat. Whether or not to salt

meat before cooking depends on which book you read. I think the general rules that apply to conventional meat cooking apply to microwave cooking as well. Do not salt meat to be roasted until after cooking. Sprinkle salt inside the cavity of poultry, if desired, and lightly salt stews and braises once the liquid has been added. Charts No. 2 and 3 serve as a quick reference, for meat, poultry and game.

Cooking Fish and Shellfish

The microwave oven excels at cooking fish. You can poach fish fillets in minutes. Arrange them in a dish in a circle with the thicker part of the fillet to the outside of the dish. If preparing a sauce to go with the fish, poach in a little white wine or water and lemon juice for a little more liquid to work with. A bay leaf, slice of onion and a few peppercorns are classic additions to the poaching liquid for extra flavour.

CHART 2 Meat, Poultry and Game (per 450g/1lb.)

	Mins. on High	Mins. on Medium	Internal Temperature Before Standing	After Standing
Beef: boned and rolled				
rare	6-7	11-13	57°C/130°F	62°C/140°F
medium	7-8	13-15	65°C/150°F	70°C/160°F
well-done	8-9	15-17	70°C/160°F	78°C/170°F
Beef: bone in				
rare	5	10	57°C/130°F	62°C/140°F
medium	6	11	65°C/150°F	70°C/160°F
well-done	8	15	70°C/160°F	78°C/170°F
Leg of Lamb	8-10	11-13	78°C/170°F	82°C/180°F
Veal	8-9	11-12	70°C/160°F	78°C/170°F
Pork	9-11	13-15	82°C/180°F	85°C/185°F
Ham				
Uncooked, boned	1st 5	15-18	55°C/130°F	70°C/160°F
Bone in	1st 5	15½-18½	55°C/130°F	70°C/160°F
Pre-cooked, boned	1st 5	12-15	55°C/130°F	
Bone in	1st 5	10-15		
Chicken	6-8	9-11	85°C/185°F	94°C/190°F
Duck	6-8	9-11	85°C/185°F	94°C/190°F
Turkey	9-11	12-15	85°C/185°F	94°C/190°F
Pheasant		20 total		
Poussins	15-20 total			
Wild Duck	5	10 total		
Pigeon	10 total			
Quail	5-9 total			

CHART 3 Small Cuts of Meat, Poultry and Game

Type	Mins. on High	Mins. on Medium	Special Instructions
Steaks (3.75mm/ 1½″ thick) 120g-180g/4-6oz			Use a browning dish pre-heated to manufacturer's instructions. Use timing for rare when cooking kebabs.
rare	2-3		
medium rare	3-4		
medium	5-7		
well-done	7-9		
Lamb Chops	7-9	13-15	Use a browning dish Cook in liquid
Lamb Fillet		10-12	Brown, then cook in liquid
Pork Chops	7-9	13-15	Use a browning dish Cook in liquid
Pork Fillet		15	Brown, then cook in liquid
Veal Chops	7-9	13-15	Use a browning dish Cook in liquid
Smoked Pork Chops	4-6		Pre-cooked and browned
Ham Steaks	3		Pre-cooked and browned
Minced/Ground Meat (450g/1lb)	5		Break up with a fork as it cooks
Hamburgers	2½-3		Use browning dish
Lamb Patties	2½-3		Use browning dish
Meatballs (675g/1½ lbs)	10-12		
Duck Portions			Use browning dish
1 Breast (boned)	6		
2 Legs		15	Brown each side first
Chicken			Brown first if desired
1 Breast		2-3	
1 Leg		3-4	
2 Pieces		3-6	
3 Pieces		4-7	
4 Pieces		7-9	
Turkey Escalopes/Cutlets		10-15	
Turkey Legs (450g/1lb)	1st 10	13-16	
Bacon		4 1	On rack or paper towels Per side on pre-heated browning dish
Sausages		2	Use browning dish

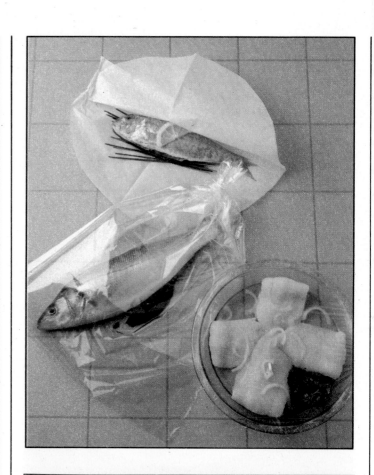

CHART 4 Fish and Shellfish (per 450g/1lb.)

Type	Mins. on high	Type	Mins. on high
Cod Steaks and Fillets	4-5	Salmon (Whole, 1kg/2.2lbs)	10-15
Halibut and Turbot Steaks and Fillets	4-5	Salmon Steaks and Tail pieces	2-7
Smoked Fish (poached)	1-2	Sea Bass (Whole, 1kg/2.2lbs)	10-15
Sole Fillets	2-3	Prawns/Shrimp Scampi/Langoustines	2-5
Mackerel	10-12	Scallops	2-5
Trout	8-10	Mussels	2-3
Herring Fillets	6-8	Oysters	1-2
Tuna Steaks	5	Squid	6
Monkfish Tail Portion Sliced	8-9 2-5		

Whole fish can be "fried" in a browning dish. They can also be cooked in bags, shallow covered dishes or enclosed in greaseproof paper — en papillote.

Shellfish can toughen if cooked too quickly at too high a temperature. Add them to a hot sauce and leave for 5 minutes to cook in residual heat. Alternatively, cook on their own for no more than 3 minutes.

See chart No. 4 for times and settings.

Cooking Vegetables

Microwave cooking is ideal for vegetables. Very little water is needed, so they keep their colour and nutrients. They are best cooked loosely covered, and whole vegetables like corn-on-the-cob, aubergines, artichokes and chicory can be completely wrapped in cling film and cooked without any water. Cooking bags are another alternative.

Break broccoli into even-sized pieces and, if cooking a large quantity, be sure to put the flower ends in toward the centre of the dish. Trim down the tough ends of asparagus and peel the ends of the stalks. This will help the stalks cook quickly before the tips are overcooked. Some vegetables, like cucumbers, spring onions and button onions cook very well in butter or margarine alone, if well covered. Chart No. 5 lists suggested cooking times.

Cooking Fruit

Poach, bake and preserve fruit with ease in a microwave oven. Sterilise jars for preserving by adding a little water and heating on High for about 2-3 minutes and then draining. Metal lids and rubbers seals are best sterilised outside the microwave oven.

CHART 5 Cooking Vegetables

Type	Quantity	Water	Mins. on High	Mins. Stdg. Time
Artichokes	4	430ml/¾pt/1½ cups	10-20	5
Asparagus	450g/1lb	140ml/¼pt/½ cup	9-12	5
Aubergine/ Eggplant	2 med.	30ml/2 tbsps	7-10	5
Beans Green, French Broad/Lima	450g/1lb	140ml/¼pt/½ cup	8 10	3 3
Beetroot/Beets Whole	2	60ml/2 fl oz/¼ cup	4-5	3
Broccoli	450g/1lb	140ml/¼ pt/½ cup	4-5	3
Brussels Sprouts	450g/1lb	60ml/2 fl oz/¼ cup	8-10	3-5
Cabbage Shredded Quartered	450g/1lb	140ml/¼ pint/½ cup	7-9 9-12	3 5
Carrots Whole Sliced	225g/8oz	140ml/¼ pint/½ cup	10 7	6 5
Cauliflower Whole Florets	450g/1lb	280ml/½ pint/1 cup 140ml/¼ pint/½ cup	11 7	3 3
Chicory	4	60ml/2 fl oz/¼ cup (water or stock)	5	3
Corn-on-the-Cob	2 ears	60ml/2 fl oz/¼ cup	6	3
Courgettes/ Zucchini	450g/1lb	60ml/2 fl oz/¼ cup	5	3
Fennel Sliced Quartered	1 bulb	280ml/½ pint/1 cup boiling water	2-8 10-12	3 3
Leeks, sliced	450g/1lb	140ml/¼ pint/½ cup	7-10	3
Mushrooms	225g/8oz	30ml/2 tbsps	2	3
Okra	225g/8oz	60ml/2 fl oz/¼ cup	4	3
Onions, small Sliced	225g/8oz 2	30ml/1 fl oz/2 tbsps 60ml/2 fl oz/¼ cup	7-8 10	3 3
Parsnips	225g/8oz	140ml/¼ pint/½ cup	8-10	3
Peas, shelled	450g/1lb	140ml/¼ pint/½ cup	10-15	5
Peapods/ Mangetout	225g/8oz	140ml/¼ pint/½ cup	3	3
Peppers	2 sliced	60ml/2 fl oz/¼ cup	3	3
Potatoes New Baked Boiled	450g/1lb 2 450g/1lb	140ml/¼ pint/½ cup 140ml/¼ pint/½ cup	10-12 9-12 6-7	5 10 5
Spinach	225g/8oz		4-5	3
Turnips	225g/8oz	60ml/2 fl oz/¼ cup	12	3

Paraffin wax for sealing jars cannot be melted in a microwave oven. The great advantages of microwave preserving are that jams and jellies can be made in small amounts and the job is much less messy and time-consuming. Whole preserved fruits and pickled vegetables can't be heated long enough to kill bacteria, so they must be kept refrigerated after bottling.

Cooking Rice, Pasta, Grains and Pulses

Rice and pasta need nearly as much cooking by microwave methods as by conventional ones. However, both pasta and rice cook without sticking together and without the chance of overcooking. This is because most of the actual cooking is accomplished during standing time. All kinds of rice and shapes of pasta benefit from being put into hot water with a pinch of salt and 5ml/1 tsp oil in a deep bowl. There is no need to cover the bowl during cooking, but, during standing time, a covering of some sort will help retain heat. Ease long spaghetti into the bowl gradually as it softens. Drain rice and pasta and rinse under hot water to remove starch. Both pasta and rice can be reheated in a microwave oven without loss of texture. Fresh pasta doesn't seem to take to the microwave oven successfully.

There is a great time saving with dried peas, beans and lentils — pulses. Cover them with water in a large bowl and heat on a High setting to bring to the boil, which takes about 10 minutes. Allow the pulses to boil for about 2 minutes and then leave to stand for one hour. This cuts out overnight soaking. The pulses will cook in about 45 minutes to one hour depending on what variety is used. This is about half the conventional cooking time. Make sure pulses are cooked completely; it can be dangerous to eat them undercooked. Refer to Chart No. 6 for cooking times.

Cooking Eggs and Cheese

When poaching eggs, always pierce the yolks with a skewer or fork to prevent them from bursting. Use individual ramekins or patty pans with a spoonful of water in each. Alternatively, bring water to the boil in a large dish and add a pinch of salt and 5ml/1 tsp vinegar to help set the egg whites. Slip the eggs in one at a time. Cook just until the whites are set. To stop the cooking and to keep the eggs from drying out, keep them in a bowl of cold water. For frying eggs, choose a browning dish, and for

Microwave ovens can cut the rising time for yeast doughs nearly in half, and a loaf of bread will bake in an astonishing 8-10 minutes.

Biscuits will not usually crisp in a microwave oven except in one with a combination setting. However, they bake to a moist, chewy texture which is just as pleasing. A batch of 3 dozen will cook in about 10 minutes.

Pastry is not as much of a problem as most people believe. Prick the base and sides of the pastry well, after lining a pie or flan dish. It is essential to bake the pastry shell "blind" — without filling — in order to dry the base. Pastry will not bake to an even brown. The exception is, of course, pastry baked in a combination oven. Pastry and filling can be baked at the same time in these ovens.

CHART 6 Cooking Rice, Pasta, Grains and Pulses

Type	Quantity	Water	Mins. on High	Mins. Stdg. Time
Brown Rice	120g/4oz/ 1 cup	570ml/1 pint/ 2 cups	20	5
White Rice (long grain)	120g/4oz/ 1 cup	570ml/1 pint/ 2 cups	10-12	5
Quick Cooking Rice	120g/4oz/ 1 cup	430ml/¾ pint/ 1½ cups	6	5
Macaroni	225g/8oz/ 3 cups	1 litre/1¾ pints/ 3½ cups	6	10
Quick Cooking Macaroni	225g/8oz/ 3 cups	1 litre/1¾ pints/ 3½ cups	3	10
Spaghetti	225g/8oz	1 litre/1¾ pints/ 3½ cups	6-10	10
Tagliatelle/Fettucine	225g/8oz	1 litre/1¾ pints/ 3½ cups	5-9	10
Pasta Shapes	225g/8oz/ 3 cups	1 litre/1¾ pints/ 3½ cups	6	10
Lasagne Ravioli Cannelloni	180g-225g/ 6oz-8oz	1 litre/1¾ pints/ 3½ cups	6	10
Barley	120g/4oz/ 1 cup	570ml/1 pint/ 2 cups	20	10
Bulgur (cracked wheat)	225g/8oz/ 2 cups	570ml/1 pint/ 2 cups boiling water	4	10
Dried Beans	180g/6oz/ 1 cup	1 litre/1¾ pints/ 3½ cups	55-60	10
Dried Peas	225g/8oz/ 3 cups	1 litre/1¾ pints/ 3½ cups	45-60	10
Lentils	225g/8oz/ 3 cups	1 litre/1¾ pints/ 3½ cups	20-25	15

NOTE: Add a pinch of salt and 5ml/1 tsp oil to grains and pasta

scrambling use a deep bowl or glass measuring jug. Always remove scrambled eggs from the oven while they are still very soft. Stir during standing time to finish cooking. Hollandaise sause is easy to make. Choose the same kind of container as for scrambled eggs and have a bowl of iced water ready. Use a medium setting and cook the sauce at short intervals, whisking vigorously in between times. Put the sauce bowl into the iced water at the first sign of curdling or briefly when it has thickened, to stop the cooking process.

Cheese will get very stringy if it overcooks or gets too hot. When preparing a cheese sauce, stir finely grated cheese into the hot sauce base and leave to stand. The cheese will melt without further cooking. Cheese toppings will not brown except in a combination oven. A medium setting is best for cheese.

Baking

Baking is one of the most surprising things a microwave oven does. Quick breads, those leavened with baking powder or soda and sour milk, rise higher than they do in a conventional oven and bake faster. If using a square or loaf dish, cover the corners with foil for part of the cooking time to keep that part of the bread or cake from drying out before the middle is cooked. Cakes also rise much higher and a single layer will bake in about 6 minutes on a medium setting.

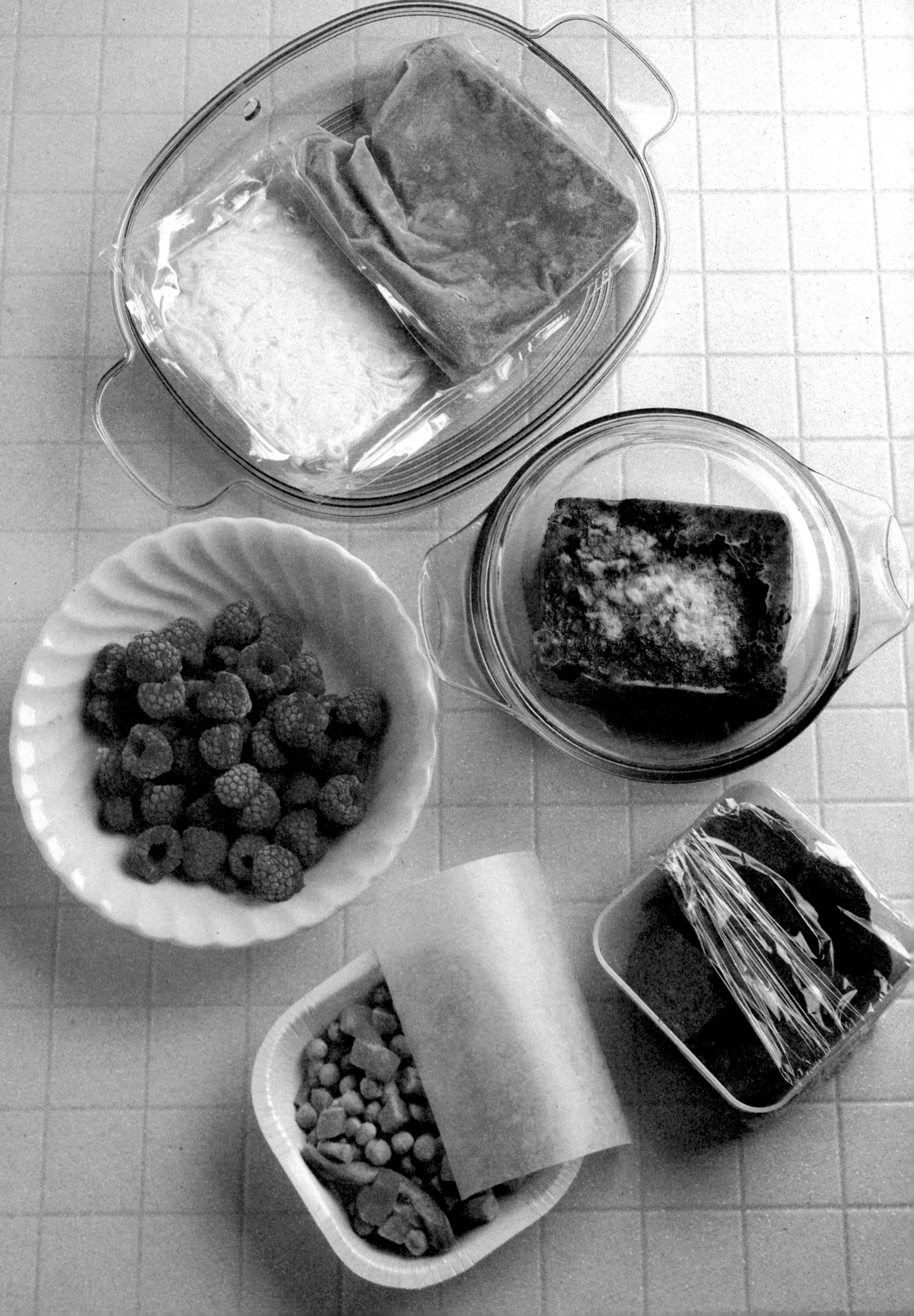

CHART 7 Reheating

	Quantity	Setting	Time from room temp. (minutes)	Special Instructions		Quantity	Setting	Time from room temp. (minutes)	Special Instructions
Spaghetti Sauce	225g/8oz 450g/1lb	Med.	5-6 7-8	Stir several times. Keep loosely covered.	Pasta	120g/4oz 225g/8oz	Med. or High	2-3 5-6	Stir once or twice. Add 5ml/ 1 tsp oil. Use shorter time for High setting.
Beef Stew	225g/8oz 450g/1lb	Med.	5-5½ 6-7	Stir occasionally. Cover loosely.	Rice	120g/4oz 225g/8oz	Med. or High	2-3 4-5	Stir once or twice. Add 5ml/ 1 tsp oil or butter. Use shorter time for High setting.
Casseroles	225g/8oz 450g/1lb	Med.	5-7 7-8	Stir occasionally. Cover loosely. Use the shorter time for chicken, fish or vegetables.	Potatoes	120g/4oz 225g/8oz 450g/1lb	High	1-2 2-3 3-4	Use the shorter time for mashed potatoes. Do not reheat fried potatoes. Cover loosely.
Chili	225g/8oz 450g/1lb	Med.	5-5½ 6-7	Stir several times. Keep loosely covered.					
Pork Chops	2 4	Med.	5 7½	Turn over halfway through. Cover loosely.	Corn-on-the-Cob	2 ears 4 ears	High	2-3 4-6	Wrap in plastic wrap/cling film
Lamb Chops	2 4	Med.	4-5 6-10	Turn over halfway through. Cover loosely.	Carrots	225g/8oz 450g/1lb	High	1-2 2-4	Cover loosely. Stir once.
Sliced beef, pork, veal	120g/4oz 225g/8oz	Med.	3-5 6-7½	Add gravy or sauce if possible. Cover loosely.	Turnips	225g/8oz 450g/1lb	High	1-2 2-4	Cover loosely. Stir carefully.
Sliced turkey, chicken, ham	120g/4oz 225g/8oz	Med.	2½-5 4-6	Add gravy or sauce if possible. Cover loosely.	Broccoli Asparagus	120g/4oz 225g/8oz	High	2 2	Cover loosely. Rearrange once.
					Peas Beans Courgettes/ Zucchini	120g/4oz 225g/8oz	High	1-1½ 1½-2	Cover loosely. Stir occasionally.

To let air and heat circulate underneath breads, cakes and pastry shells, place them on a rack or inverted saucer. This allows the base to cook faster and more evenly. Once baked and cool, keep microwave-baked goods well covered. They seem to dry out faster than those conventionally baked.

Defrosting and Reheating

With the defrosting and reheating abilities of a microwave oven menu planning can become crisis-free. Most ovens incorporate an automatic defrosting control into their setting programs. If your oven does not have this facility, use the lowest temperature setting and employ an on/off technique. In other words, turn the oven on at 30 second-1 minute intervals and let the food stand for a minute or two before repeating the process. This procedure allows the food to defrost evenly without starting to cook at the edges. The times given in Charts No. 7 and 8 apply to ovens of 600-700 watts.

Always cover the food when defrosting or reheating. Plastic containers, plastic bags and freezer-to-table ware can be used to freeze and defrost food in. Meals can be placed on paper or plastic trays and frozen. Cover with cling film or greaseproof paper. Usually, foods are better defrosted first and cooked or reheated second. There are exceptions to this rule, so be sure to check instructions on pre-packaged foods before proceeding. Food frozen in blocks, such as spinach or casseroles, should be broken up as they defrost.

Breads, rolls and coffee cakes can be placed on paper plates or covered in paper towels to reheat or defrost. These materials will help protect the foods and absorb moisture which will come to the surface and could make these foods soggy. If you want a crisp crust on reheated bread, slip a sheet of foil under the paper towel and don't cover completely.

When reheating foods in a sauce, stir occasionally to distribute heat evenly. Spread food out in an even layer for uniform heating. Sauces and gravies can be poured over sliced meat and poultry to keep it moist while reheating. Vegetables, except for root vegetables and starchy ones like corn, lose texture when they are reheated. It is best to add them at the last

CHART 8 Defrosting

	Mins. on Low/Defrost Setting per 450g/1lb	Mins. Stdg. Time	Instructions
Pork, Veal, Lamb, Beef for Roasting	8-10	30-40	Pierce covering. Turn frequently.
Ground/ Minced Beef or Lamb	7-8	5-6	Pierce wrapping. Break up as it defrosts.
Hamburgers	6-8	5	Use shorter time if individually wrapped. Pierce wrapper and separate when starting to defrost. Turn patties over once.
Bacon	6-8	5	Cover in paper towels. Separate as slices defrost.
Sausages	6-8	5	Cover in paper towels. Separate as defrosting.
Whole Chickens, Duck, Game Birds	5-7	30	Pierce wrapper. Remove giblets as soon as possible. Cover leg ends, wings, breast bone with foil part of the time. Turn several times.
Poultry Pieces	6-8	15-20	Pierce wrapper. Turn several times.
Casseroles, filled crêpes (for 4 people)	4-10	10	Defrost in dish, loosely covered. Stir casseroles if possible.

	Mins. on Low/Defrost Setting per 450g/1lb	Mins. Stdg. Time	Instructions
Vegetables	1-8	3-5	Cover loosely. Break up or stir occasionally.
Fish Fillets and Steaks	6-10	5-10	Pierce wrapper. Separate during defrosting. Use greater time for steaks.
Whole Fish	6-8	10	Pierce wrapper. Turn over during defrosting. Cover tail with foil halfway through.
Shellfish	6-8	6	Pierce wrapper. Stir or break up pieces during defrosting.
Bread Loaf	2-4 (per average loaf)	5-10	Cover with paper towels. Turn over once.
1 Slice Bread	20 seconds	1	Cover in paper towels.
Rolls 6 12	1½-3 2-4	3 5	Cover in paper towels. Turn over once.
Cake	1½-2	2	Place on serving plate. Some icings not suitable.
Fruit Pie 23cm/9″	8-10	6	Use a glass dish. Place on inverted saucer or rack.

minute to other foods. To tell if reheating is completed, touch the bottom of the plate or container. If it feels hot, then the food is ready.

Foods can be arranged on plates in advance and reheated very successfully, an advantage when entertaining. With a microwave oven, you can spend more time with your guests than by yourself in the kitchen!

Recipe Conversion

Experiment with your favourite recipes and you will probably find that many of them can be converted for microwave cooking with only a few changes. Things that don't work are recipes which call for whipped egg whites, such as angel food cake and crisp meringue shells. Soft meringues for pies will work, and one of the most amazing recipe conversions is that for crisp meringues. These meringues triple in size as they cook and are made from a fondant-like mixture.

Batters for pancakes, waffles or Yorkshire pudding are impossible to cook successfully. Deep fat frying is understandably impossible. Yeast doughs and biscuit doughs must be specially formulated for microwave cooking. To convert your own recipes, the following rules will help:

* Look for similar microwave recipes with the same quantities of solid ingredients, dish size, techniques and times.

* Reduce liquid quantities by one quarter. More can always be added later in cooking.

* Cut down on fat and save calories as well as cooking time. Fat will attract microwave energy and slow down the cooking of the other ingredients in the recipe.

* Reduce the seasoning in your recipe; microwave cooking intensifies flavours.

* Microwave cooking takes approximately a quarter of the time of conventional cooking. Allow at least 5 minutes standing time before checking to see if the food is cooked. You can always add more time at this point if necessary.

Microwave
THE RECIPES

Microwave HERBS & SPICES

INTRODUCTION

The use of herbs and spices to enhance the flavour of food is not a new idea. For centuries they have been used to make food more exciting and palatable. With the use of the microwave you can now make delicious, tasty dishes in double quick time.

Herb cookery is particularly suited to the microwave, as the quick cooking time does not impair the flavour of even the most delicate herbs. The recipes in this book have been tested using fresh herbs; if these are not available use dried, but remember that they have a more concentrated flavour so use only $1/3$-$1/2$ of the quantity stated. As well as cooking herbs, the microwave can be used to dry many herbs, with excellent results. Try parsley, chives, bergamot, the mints, lemon balm, marjoram, oregano, sage, tarragon, thyme and rosemary – they will have a much better colour and flavour than when dried naturally. Dry herbs in small quantities, about 15g/$1/2$ oz at a time, on a double sheet of absorbent paper. Cook on HIGH for 2-4 minutes, turning and repositioning every minute; they are ready when they are just crisp. Store them crumbled or whole.

Spices have the best flavour when ground just before use, but if this is not convenient, make sure you buy good quality spices in small quantities. Both dried herbs and spices should be kept in airtight containers in a cool, dry place. If they have lost their aroma they will have lost their flavour, too, so discard and buy fresh.

The following glossary should help you to become familiar with the herbs and spices used in the book, but don't be afraid to experiment yourself – herb and spice cookery should be fun.

Allspice – Whole berries or in ground form, with the taste of nutmeg, cloves and cinnamon combined. Use in pâtés, pickles, stews and curries, marinades for meat, poultry and fish, with cheese, in baking and in puddings/desserts.

Aniseed – A native of the Middle East, now grown in south eastern Europe, North Africa, India and parts of Latin America. Spicy sweet liquorice flavour, used in sweet and savoury dishes. Use with all meats, especially curries, poultry, fish and fruit.

Basil – Fresh or dried leaves with a mild liquorice taste. The herb is native to Italy, France and Egypt, but grows easily elsewhere. Especially good with tomatoes and garlic. Use in all savoury Italian dishes, as well as in stews and with chicken, fish, seafood, cheese, eggs and sauces, pasta and pizza. Use raw in salads.

Bay leaf – Leaf of the sweet laurel tree. Native to southern Europe, but can easily be grown as an evergreen in home gardens anywhere. One of the ingredients of the classic bouquet garni. Use in stews and curries, soups and sauces, marinades for meat, poultry and fish, and also in poaching liquids for poultry and fish. Gives interesting taste to pickles and preserves. Remove before serving.

Bergamot – Fresh herb native to North America and Europe. Use with meats, poultry and game. Plant has vivid red flowers that can be used as a tea.

Borage – Native to eastern Europe. Both the flower and leaves have a slight cucumber flavour. Add to salad, soups, cheese and eggs.

Cardamom – Whole pods or ground spice with a sweet, lemony taste. Native to India, Ceylon and Guatemala. Whole pods can be green, brown, black or white. White cardamom is bleached and does not have as much flavour. Crush pods slightly before use to release more flavour, or use only the seeds inside. Ground cardamom is usually expensive. Use in curries and lamb dishes, with rice and in puddings/desserts.

Caraway seed – Cultivated in parts of Europe, southern Mediterranean and the USA. Closely related to fennel and dill, can be used in both sweet and-savoury dishes. Add to salads, especially coleslaw, red cabbage, bread, cakes and biscuits.

Cassia bark – Closely related to cinnamon; sold as quills, pieces or ground. Cassia is stronger and more bitter than cinnamon so is often reserved for savoury foods. Use in curries, stews, casseroles and rice. Remove before serving.

Cayenne pepper – Made from the fruit and seed of the 'bird chili'. Very pungent, though not as hot as some chili powders. Use with fish, shellfish, chicken, cheese and eggs.

Celery seed – Small brown seeds that are sometimes ground and mixed with salt for celery salt. Native to India, Turkey and Egypt. Use in pickles, with eggs and cheese, with rice and pasta, with vegetables and in salad dressings.

Chervil – A fresh herb with delicate flavour and fragile leaves. Use in soups, salads and egg dishes.

Chilies – Fresh or dried, whole or crushed. Native to Central and South America, India and the Far East. Available fresh, red or green. Green chilies are the hotter of the two and the seeds are the hottest part. Mild red varieties are ground for paprika, hot for cayenne pepper. Use sparingly in meat dishes such as curries and chili con carne, and with chicken, fish, eggs, cheese, rice and pasta. Always wash hands well after handling.

Chinese five spice powder – Used in many authentic Chinese dishes. Available ready made, it consists of ground anise, cassia bark, cloves, fennel and star anise.

Chives – Slender green herb with an onion taste. Originally from Denmark, but now grown in many countries. Good in any savoury dish and in salads and dressings. Use as an attractive garnish.

Cinnamon – Stick or ground spice from Ceylon and the Seychelle Islands with a sweet, strong taste. Use with meat and poultry, with curries and stews. Most frequent use is in desserts and puddings. Use whole sticks in pickling and preserving, and with poached fruit. Remove stick before serving. Rinsed and dried, sticks can be reused several times.

Cloves – Whole or ground spice from Zanzibar and Madagascar, with very strong, aromatic taste. Use with all meat, especially ham and pork, with chicken and in fish dishes such as marinated herring, in curries, sauces and pilau rice. Most frequently used in sweet dishes and baked goods and in pickles and preserves.

Coriander – Spice is in seed or ground form and has a sweet, orange flavour. Leaves are used as a herb and look like flat Italian parsley, but have a very strong taste. Native to Central and South America, the Mediterranean, France, Morocco and Rumania. Also cultivated in India and Indonesia. Use in seed or ground form in stews and curries, rice, pilaffs, with chicken, cheese and eggs. Also used in sweet dishes. If using seeds, crush slightly to release more flavour. Use in leaf form like any herb, but especially in curries or Moroccan stews. Finely chopped leaves are the prominent flavour in Mexican salsas.

Cumin – Seed or ground spice. Very pungent and aromatic. Origin was Mediterranean, but also native to Middle East, India and Turkey. Use in curries, Mexican dishes, marinades, chutneys, with cheese and egg dishes and grilled/broiled meats, such as kebabs.

Curry powder – Mixture of several ground spices such as turmeric, cumin, coriander, fenugreek, cayenne pepper and dehydrated ground garlic. Convenient, but not as flavourful as using individual spices. In addition to curries, use in chutneys, salad dressings and egg and cheese dishes.

Dill – Seed or fresh and dried weed. Native to Europe and the United States. Seed has a flavour similar to caraway or anise. Especially good with fish, eggs and cheese. Also use in baking, in pickles, with vegetables and in salad dressings. Fresh dill weed makes an attractive garnish.

Fennel – Seed, or fresh tops or weed with a mild liquorice taste. Native to Europe and India. Green tops of the Florentine fennel bulb can be used as a herb. Seeds are usually pale green. Use in Italian dishes, in curries and in sausage meat. Especially good with fish.

Fenugreek – Seed or ground spice. One of the ingredients in curry powder. Native to Europe, Morocco and India. Has a very strong, slightly bitter taste. Mostly used in curries.

Fines herbes – a mixture of herbs used in classic French cuisine. It consists of equal quantities of chervil, chives, tarragon and parsley.

Garam masala – Literally 'hot spices', this is an essential in Indian cookery. Use with meat, poultry, fish, rice, eggs, some vegetables and especially in curries.

Garlic – Fresh bulbs or dried powder, granules or salt. Pungent and highly aromatic. Native to southern Europe and countries with warm climates. Essential in curries and Mediterranean dishes. Use in chutneys, with eggs and cheese, rice, pasta and shellfish. Fresh garlic is the best form to use, however, 1.25ml/¼ tsp garlic powder or granules is equal to 1 clove fresh garlic.

Ginger – Fresh root or ground. Native to Indonesia, India, Nigeria. Hot, peppery taste with slight sweetness. Peel and grate, chop or slice the fresh root. Use in curries and Oriental dishes. Especially good with pork, ham and chicken. Use in preserves and desserts/puddings.

Herbes de Provence – Dried mixture of thyme, basil, savory, fennel and lavender flowers. Use with vegetables, all meats and fish, in sauces and stews with a Mediterranean influence.

Horseradish – Native to Europe and Asia. Use grated or as a sauce with fish, chicken, egg and vegetables.

Hyssop – A native herb of central and southern Europe. It is an ancient herb and is mentioned several times in the Bible. Slight minty taste, use in soups, salads, and stews – especially lamb. Traditionally added to cranberries, stewed peaches and apricots.

Juniper berries – Fruit of an evergreen, native of Europe. Use with meat, poultry, game and cabbage. Also add to pâtés.

Lemon balm – Native to the Mediterranean, the aromatic leaves have a strong lemon scent when crushed. Used chopped in stuffings, salads and desserts. Use whole to garnish fruit dishes.

Lemon grass – Native to Thailand and the Far East. Peel the outer layers and chop the core. Use in Indonesian and Oriental cooking.

Lemon thyme – Delicate lemon flavour, goes particularly well with chicken and fish.

Lovage – Native to the Mediterranean, but can be grown elsewhere. Robust flavour similar to celery. Use in stuffings, stews, soups and with fish.

Mace – Available as blades or ground. Tastes and smells similar to nutmeg, but is much stronger and should be used sparingly. Best kept for savoury dishes, especially soups, sauces and casseroles. Can be used in milk puddings.

Marjoram – Fresh or dried herb. Asian and European origin. Similar taste to oregano. Use in all savoury dishes. Young leaves can be used whole as a garnish or raw in salads.

Mint – Fresh or dried herb. Very fragrant and sweet in its many varieties. Grown in most countries. Especially good with lamb. Use with carrots, cucumbers, peas and new potatoes. Good in fruit desserts. Fresh is preferable to dried.

Mustard – There are three varieties of mustard: white, black and brown. English mustard is made from a blend of white and black mustard seeds with a little wheat flour and turmeric. Use whole seeds to flavour milk for sauces and for pickling, and in spice mixtures for meat and seafood.

Nutmeg – Whole berries or pre-grated spice. Native to Indonesia and West Indies. Sweet, aromatic and slightly nutty taste. Use sparingly in stews and sauces (especially cheese). Good in curries and with pork and veal. Generally reserved for desserts/puddings and baking.

Oregano – Fresh or dried (most common). Strong and pungent. Use in Italian and Spanish cooking. Good with all meats, rice, pasta and egg dishes. Essential on pizzas.

Paprika – Ground. Native to Hungary and Spain. Use with all meats and poultry. Add to cheese sauces and scrambled eggs. Essential in goulash and many eastern European dishes. Sprinkle onto casseroles, vegetables or fish as a garnish.

Parsley – Fresh or dried herb. Grown in all countries with a temperate climate. Use in stuffings, in all meat, poultry and fish dishes, sauces of all kinds and salad dressings. Use chopped or whole in salads and whole as a garnish. Flat-leafed variety has more flavour than curly-leafed. Fresh is easily available and much better than dried.

Peppercorns – Black, white, green and pink. Native to India, Brazil, Ceylon and Malaysia. Use black and white peppercorns ground as a basic seasoning. Crush the black or green peppercorns roughly for steak au poivre. Add whole to marinades or poaching liquids. Green peppercorns are fresh, unripe berries. Black are ripened and dried. White are ripened, soaked and skinned. Pink are usually preserved in vinegar. Use in all meat, poultry and fish dishes, with cheese and eggs, vegetables, rice and pasta.

Rosemary – Fragrant fresh or dried herb. Native to Europe. Grows to a large, evergreen shrub. Good with all meats, poultry and vegetables.

Saffron – Strands or powder from the stigmas of crocus flowers. Native to Italy, Spain and Portugal. Strands are expensive and powder less so, however, not much is needed to give a golden yellow colour to rice dishes like risotto and paella. Also used in delicate seafood sauces and baked goods.

Sage – Fresh or dried herb. Native to Europe. Good with pork, poultry and game. Ingredient in stuffings. Also used with cheese and eggs. Flavour is very strong; use sparingly.

Salad burnet – Fresh herb which grows wild in many parts of Europe. Does not dry well and requires minimal cooking. Use in soups, salads and as a attractive garnish.

Savory – Fresh or dried herb. Native to Europe. Summer and winter varieties. Use with meats, poultry, fish, eggs and fruit. Good in soups and salads.

Star anise – Native to China and Japan, but also grown in the Philippines. It is a component of Chinese five spice powder. Use in Chinese cookery, with fish, shellfish, rice, pork and chicken.

Tansy – Quite bitter in flavour, so best used sparingly. Traditional herb at Easter added to puddings, custards and cakes. Also good with fish, eggs and cheese dishes.

Tarragon – Fresh or dried herb. French tarragon has a slight anise flavour. Russian tarragon looks the same but has less flavour. Was native to Siberia, but cultivated in France and Yugoslavia. Use with chicken, fish, eggs, game and vegetables. Classic ingredient in Bernaise sauce. Also use in vinegar and for salad dressings.

Thyme – Fresh or dried herb. Native to Europe and all temperate climates. Small, dark green leaves with pungent aroma. Use with all meat, poultry, game, fish dishes and vegetables. Add to rice and pasta, sauces, soups and stuffings.

Turmeric – Ground spice. Native to India, the Caribbean, Middle East, Africa, Ceylon. Gives curry powder its yellow colour. Use in rice dishes and with seafood. Can be used as a saffron substitute.

All the recipes in this book were prepared in an oven with a 700 watt maximum output. For 500 watt ovens add 40 seconds for each minute stated in the recipe. For 600 watt ovens add 20 seconds for each minute stated in the recipe. If using a 650 watt oven only a slight increase in overall time is necessary.

SOUPS & STARTERS

Celery Cheese Dip with Chervil

PREPARATION TIME: 10 minutes

MICROWAVE COOKING TIME:
5-7 minutes

SERVES: 4-6 people

1 stick celery, finely chopped
15g/½ oz/1 tbsp butter
60g/2oz/½ cup Port Salut or St. Paulin
cheese, grated
140ml/¼ pint/½ cup natural yogurt
1 slice ham, finely chopped
15ml/1 tbsp chopped chervil

Put the celery and the butter in a small bowl and cook, uncovered, on HIGH for 3-4 minutes until tender but still slightly crunchy. Add the cheese and cook on HIGH for 2-4 minutes until melted, stirring frequently. Stir in the yogurt, chervil and ham. Chill thoroughly. Serve with sticks of raw vegetables or strips of pitta bread.

Swiss Cheese Layer

PREPARATION TIME: 5 minutes

MICROWAVE COOKING TIME:
3-5 minutes

SERVES: 4 people

120g/4oz/1 cup grated Emmental cheese
15ml/1 tbsp chopped borage
4 eggs
Salt and pepper
120g/4oz/1 cup grated Gruyère cheese
10ml/2 tsps savory
30g/1oz/¼ cup cornchips, crushed

Mix the Emmental cheese and borage together and divide between 4 ramekins/custard cups. Crack 1 egg into each dish and season to taste with salt and pepper. Mix the Gruyère cheese with the savory and top each dish with the cheese. Sprinkle with the crushed corn chips, arrange in a circle and cook on LOW for 3-5 minutes until the cheese melts and the eggs are cooked.

Celery Cheese Dip with Chervil (top) and Swiss Cheese Layer (bottom).

Courgette/Zucchini Soup with Peppermint

PREPARATION TIME: 20 minutes

MICROWAVE COOKING TIME: 17-20 minutes

SERVES: 4 people

15ml/1 tbsp oil
1 medium onion, peeled and finely chopped
1 small clove garlic, peeled and crushed
2 medium potatoes, peeled and diced
675g/1½ lbs courgettes/zucchini, finely sliced
1150ml/2 pints/4 cups hot chicken stock
Salt
Freshly ground black pepper
2 eggs
15ml/1 tbsp grated Parmesan cheese
15ml/1 tbsp chopped peppermint
Pinch nutmeg

GARNISH
Fresh peppermint leaves
60ml/4 tbsps double/heavy cream (optional)

Put the oil, onion and garlic in a large bowl. Cook, uncovered, on HIGH for 2-3 minutes to soften, then add the potatoes and cook on HIGH for 2 minutes. Add the courgettes/zucchini and cook on HIGH for 3-4 minutes. Stir in the stock, salt and pepper. Cover and cook for 5-15 minutes until the vegetables are soft. Purée in a blender or food processor and return to the bowl. Beat the eggs, cheese, peppermint and nutmeg together. Gradually add to the soup, whisking continuously. Cook, uncovered, on HIGH for 3-5 minutes or until hot, stirring once. Serve garnished with the peppermint leaves and/or a swirl of cream.

Hot Tomato Salad

PREPARATION TIME: 5 minutes

MICROWAVE COOKING TIME: 2-3 minutes

SERVES: 4 people

2 large beef tomatoes (total weight about 560g/1¼ lbs)

45ml/3 tbsps olive oil
15ml/1 tbsp cider vinegar
5ml/1 tsp chopped chives
5ml/1 tsp roughly chopped basil
2.5ml/½ tsp whole grain mustard

Slice the tomatoes and arrange on a micro-proof serving dish or on four individual dishes. Mix the oil, vinegar, chives, basil and mustard in a small jug and pour over the tomatoes. Cook, uncovered, on HIGH for 2-3 minutes until hot but not cooked. If using individual dishes, arrange these in a circle in the microwave. Serve immediately.

Cod and Mushroom Vol-au-Vents

PREPARATION TIME: 10 minutes

MICROWAVE COOKING TIME: 6-9 minutes

MAKES: 18

180g/6oz smoked cod
30g/1oz/2 tbsps butter

This page: Courgette/Zucchini Soup with Peppermint. Facing page: Hot Tomato Salad (top) and Cod and Mushroom Vol-au-Vents (bottom).

60g/2oz mushrooms, finely sliced
30g/1oz/2 tbsps flour
140ml/¼ pint/½ cup milk
5ml/1 tsp chopped savory
10ml/2 tsps chopped chives
18 vol-au-vent cases/patty shells, cooked

Put the fish in a shallow dish, cover and cook on HIGH for 2 minutes and set aside. Put the butter in a small bowl with the mushrooms, cover and cook on HIGH for 1 minute until the mushrooms are soft. Gently stir in the flour and add the milk and the herbs. Cook on HIGH for 2-3 minutes until thickened, stirring frequently. Flake the fish into the sauce, divide the mixture between the pastry cases and arrange 6 at a time in a circle on paper towels. Cook on HIGH for 30 seconds-1 minute to reheat. Repeat with remaining vol-au-vents.

Microwave
COOKING WITH HERBS

MEAT & FISH DISHES

Turkey Marsala

PREPARATION TIME: 15 minutes

MICROWAVE COOKING TIME:
22-29 minutes

SERVES: 4 people

4 120g/4oz turkey breast fillets
1 small onion, peeled and finely chopped
1 red pepper, seeded and sliced
1 clove garlic, peeled and crushed
15ml/1 tbsp oil
225g/8oz mushrooms, quartered
140ml/¼ pint/½ cup good hot chicken
    stock
70ml/4½ tbsps Marsala
30ml/2 tsps lemon verbena or lemon
    thyme
15ml/1 tbsp salad burnet
15ml/1 tbsp cornflour/cornstarch
Salt
Freshly ground black pepper

Cut the turkey into thin slivers. Put
the onion, pepper, garlic and the oil
in a casserole and cook on HIGH for
3 minutes, until just beginning to
soften. Add the turkey and cook on
HIGH for 6 minutes, until almost
cooked. Add the mushrooms and stir
in the stock, marsala and herbs.
Cover and cook on HIGH for 10-15
minutes until the meat is cooked and
tender. Mix the cornflour/cornstarch
with 45ml/3 tbsps water and stir into
the casserole. Cook, uncovered, on
HIGH for 3-5 minutes until
thickened, stirring twice. Season to
taste with salt and pepper.

**This page: Turkey Marsala (top)
and Chicken and Lemon Parcels
(bottom). Facing page: Chicken
with Sausage Meat Stuffing.**

Chicken with Sausage Meat Stuffing

PREPARATION TIME: 15 minutes	
MICROWAVE COOKING TIME: 34 minutes	
SERVES: 4 people	

STUFFING
225g/8oz pork sausage meat
60g/2oz/½ cup crushed bran flakes
30ml/2 tbsps chopped mixed herbs
15ml/1 tbsp chopped parsley
*30g/1oz/2 tbsps grated fresh coconut or
    desiccated coconut*
1 egg
Salt
Freshly ground black pepper
1½ kg/3lbs chicken
*5ml/1 tsp soy sauce mixed with 15ml/
    1 tbsp water*

Put all the stuffing ingredients into a bowl and mix well. Carefully lift the skin of the chicken away from the breast and body. Stuff the sausage meat between the skin and the chicken and spread out as evenly as possible. Place the chicken on a rack in a dish and brush with the soy sauce and water mixture. Cover with roasting film or a roasting bag which has been split open. Cook on HIGH for 10 minutes, then reduce setting and cook on MEDIUM for 24 minutes, or until the chicken is cooked. Shield the breast of the chicken with a small piece of foil for the last 10 minutes of cooking.

Chicken and Lemon Parcels

PREPARATION TIME: 20 minutes	
MICROWAVE COOKING TIME: 10-15 minutes	
SERVES: 4 people	

4 180-225g/4-6oz chicken breast fillets
15ml/1 tbsp oil
1 small onion, peeled and finely chopped
120g/4oz mushrooms, finely chopped
10ml/2 tsps chopped tarragon
Salt
Freshly ground black pepper
60g/2oz/4 tbsps unsalted butter
1 egg yolk
15ml/1 tbsp lemon juice
15ml/1 tbsp single/light cream

Flatten the chicken breasts between 2 sheets of greaseproof/wax paper using a rolling pin, taking care to keep the chicken in one piece. Set aside. Put the oil and onion together in a small bowl. Cover and cook on HIGH for 2 minutes to soften. Add the mushrooms and half of the chopped tarragon, cover and cook on HIGH for 1-2 minutes. Season to taste with salt and pepper. Divide the mixture between each chicken breast and fold up to form parcels. Arrange in a circle in a dish and cook, uncovered, on HIGH for 6-8 minutes. Transfer to a serving dish and keep warm. Meanwhile, put the butter in a small bowl and cook, uncovered, on HIGH for 1 minute or until melted. Mix the lemon juice, cream and egg yolk together and pour onto the butter; whisk. Cook on HIGH for 30 seconds-1 minute, whisking every 20 seconds until thickened. Pour the sauce over the chicken parcels to serve.

Veal and Garlic Cheese Rolls

PREPARATION TIME: 10 minutes	
MICROWAVE COOKING TIME: 8-10 minutes	
SERVES: 4 people	

4 120-180g/4-6oz veal escalopes
2 small cloves garlic, peeled and crushed
225g/8oz low fat, soft cheese
Small bunch chives, chopped
Salt
Freshly ground black pepper
5ml/1 tsp paprika (optional)

Flatten the veal escalopes between 2 sheets of greaseproof/wax paper using a rolling pin and taking care to keep in one piece. Set aside.

Combine the garlic, cheese and chives together and season with salt and pepper. Divide the mixture into 4, spread over each of the veal escalopes and roll up like a Swiss roll/jelly roll. Sprinkle with paprika if desired. Arrange in a circle in a dish and cook, uncovered, on HIGH for 8-10 minutes. Serve immediately.

Liver Casserole

PREPARATION TIME: 15 minutes	
MICROWAVE COOKING TIME: 15-20 minutes	
SERVES: 4 people	

30g/1oz/2 tbsps butter
2 large onions, peeled and sliced
1 small clove garlic, peeled and crushed
675g/1½ lbs lamb's liver, sliced
30ml/2 tbsps cornflour/cornstarch
30ml/2 tbsps Cointreau
280ml/½ pint/1 cup hot beef stock
15ml/1 tbsp chopped lovage
Salt
Pepper

GARNISH
Orange slices

Put the butter, onion and garlic in a casserole and cook on HIGH for 2 minutes, until soft. Toss the liver in the mixture until well coated. Cover and cook on MEDIUM for 10-15 minutes until just cooked. Blend the cornflour/cornstarch with the Cointreau and add to the liver along with the beef stock; stir in the lovage. Season to taste. Cover and cook on HIGH for 3-4 minutes until the sauce is hot and thickened.

Facing page: Liver Casserole (top) and Veal and Garlic Cheese Rolls (bottom).

Beef Casserole with Herb Dumplings

PREPARATION TIME: 15 minutes

MICROWAVE COOKING TIME:
16-23 minutes

SERVES: 4 people

5ml/1 tsp oil
1 medium onion, peeled and finely
  chopped
340g/12oz minced/ground beef
30g/1oz/2 tbsps plain/all-purpose flour
140ml/¼ pint/½ cup beef stock
15ml/1 tbsp tomato purée/paste
Salt
Freshly ground black pepper

HERB DUMPLINGS
180g/6oz/1½ cups plain/all-purpose
  flour
2.5ml/½ tsp baking powder
Pinch dry mustard
60g/2oz/4 tbsps margarine
2.5ml/½ tsp chopped oregano
2.5ml/½ tsp chopped thyme
2.5ml/½ tsp chopped marjoram
Approx. 70ml/4½ tbsps milk

Put the oil and the onion in a casserole and cook on HIGH for 3 minutes until soft. Add the beef and cook on HIGH for 3-5 minutes, stirring occasionally. Stir in the flour, stock, tomato purée/paste and seasoning. To make the dumplings: sift the flour, baking powder, mustard and a pinch of salt into a mixing bowl. Rub in the margarine until the mixture resembles fine breadcrumbs. Stir in the herbs. Add the milk gradually and mix to form a soft dough. Divide the dough into eight balls. Arrange around the edge of the casserole. Cover and cook on LOW for 10-15 minutes until dumplings are cooked.

Pork and Orange Casserole

PREPARATION TIME: 15 minutes

MICROWAVE COOKING TIME:
16-23 minutes

SERVES: 4 people

15ml/1 tbsp oil
1 medium onion, peeled and finely sliced
450g/1lb pork – cut into 1.25cm/½ inch
  cubes
280ml/½ pint/1 cup hot chicken stock
140ml/¼ pint/½ cup unsweetened orange
  juice
5ml/1 tsp oregano – roughly chopped
10ml/2 tsps basil – roughly chopped
1 orange, peeled and sliced
30ml/2 tbsps cornflour/cornstarch
60ml/4 tbsps water

Put the oil and onion into a large casserole and cook on HIGH for 2 minutes to soften. Add the pork and cook on HIGH for 4-6 minutes, until almost cooked. Add the stock, orange juice, herbs and orange slices and stir. Mix the cornflour/cornstarch with the water and add to the casserole. Cover and cook on MEDIUM for 10-15 minutes, until the meat is completely cooked and the liquid is thickened slightly, stirring occasionally. Serve with rice.

This page: Pork and Orange Casserole. Facing page: Beef Casserole with Herb Dumplings.

Casseroled Lamb

PREPARATION TIME: 15 minutes

MICROWAVE COOKING TIME:
35 minutes

SERVES: 4 people

450g/1lb lamb fillet, cubed
15ml/1 tbsp oil
1 large onion, peeled and sliced
1 small clove garlic, peeled and crushed
30g/1oz/2 tbsps flour
225g/8oz courgettes/zucchini, sliced
225g/8oz carrots, peeled and sliced
430ml/¾ pint/1½ cups good hot beef
    stock

280ml/½ pint/1 cup brown ale
30ml/2 tbsps chopped lemon thyme
15ml/1 tbsp chopped chervil
Salt
Freshly ground black pepper

Heat a large browning dish for the manufacturer's recommended time. Meanwhile, toss the lamb in the oil. When the dish is hot, add the meat and cook on HIGH for 2-3 minutes, stirring once. Add the onion and the garlic and cook on HIGH for 2 minutes, stir in the flour and add the remaining ingredients. Cover and cook on HIGH for 10 minutes then reduce setting and cook on

MEDIUM for 20 minutes, stirring occasionally until the vegetables and meat are tender.

Stuffed Bacon Chops

PREPARATION TIME: 10 minutes

MICROWAVE COOKING TIME:
8-9 minutes

SERVES: 4 people

4 thick bacon chops
15ml/1 tbsp oil
1 small onion, peeled and finely chopped
30g/1oz macadamia nuts, chopped
120g/4oz/¾ cup cooked rice
30g/1oz/¼ cup dried prunes, stones
    removed and chopped
15ml/1 tbsp chopped sage
Freshly ground black pepper
Salt
30g/1oz/2 tbsps butter

Carefully cut a slit down the side of each bacon chop. Put the oil, onion and nuts in a small bowl and cook, uncovered, on HIGH for 2 minutes. Stir in the rice, prunes, sage, salt and pepper. Cover and cook on HIGH for 2-4 minutes until hot. Pack the stuffing into each chop. Heat a browning dish according to the manufacturer's instructions. Add the butter and quickly add the chops, press down slightly and turn browned side up. Cook, uncovered, on HIGH for 4 minutes or until cooked. Serve with a salad or green vegetables.

**This page: Stuffed Bacon Chops.
Facing page: Herb Lamb Noisettes
(top) and Casseroled Lamb
(bottom).**

Herb Lamb Noisettes

PREPARATION TIME: 10 minutes

MICROWAVE COOKING TIME:
11 minutes

SERVES: 4 people

1 large onion, peeled and chopped
15ml/1 tbsp oil
1 210g/7oz can chopped tomatoes
1 small clove garlic, peeled and crushed
5ml/1 tsp marjoram
5ml/1 tsp oregano
120g/4oz button mushrooms
4 120g/4oz noisettes of lamb
Knob butter

Put the onion and oil in a small bowl and cook on HIGH for 3 minutes, until soft. Add the tomatoes, garlic, herbs and mushrooms. Cook, uncovered, on HIGH for 3 minutes, stirring once. Set aside and keep warm. Heat a large browning dish for the manufacturer's recommended time. Add the butter and quickly place the noisettes in the dish and press each one down firmly, turn over and press down again. Cook on HIGH for 5 minutes. Transfer the noisettes to a warm serving dish and, if necessary, reheat the sauce for 1 minute on HIGH. Serve the sauce poured over the noisettes.

Smoky Haddock and Chive au Gratin

PREPARATION TIME: 10 minutes

MICROWAVE COOKING TIME:
5-8 minutes

SERVES: 4 people

340g/12oz smoked haddock, skinned
140ml/¼ pint/½ cup white wine
Bayleaf
120g/4oz mushrooms, sliced
30g/1oz/2 tbsps butter
30g/1oz/2 tbsps flour
140ml/¼ pint/½ cup milk
Small bunch chives, chopped
60g/2 oz/½ cup Cheddar cheese, grated
15ml/1 tbsp chopped parsley

60ml/4 tbsps brown breadcrumbs

Place the haddock in a shallow dish with the wine, bay leaves and mushrooms. Cover and cook on HIGH for 3 minutes until the fish is cooked. Set aside. Put the butter in a small bowl and cook on HIGH for 30 seconds. Stir in the flour and cook on HIGH for 30 seconds. Add the cooking liquor from the fish together with the milk and mix well. Cook on HIGH for 2-4 minutes, whisking every minute until thickened. Add the mushrooms, chives and fish, flaking the fish slightly as you do so, and mix well. Divide between four individual gratin dishes. Sprinkle over the cheese, parsley and breadcrumbs and cook on HIGH for 1-2 minutes or brown under the grill/broiler.

Plaice with Herbed Mushrooms

PREPARATION TIME: 20 minutes

MICROWAVE COOKING TIME:
11-14 minutes

SERVES: 4 people

4 large plaice fillets
15g/½ oz/1 tbsp butter
Small clove garlic, peeled and crushed
1 small onion, peeled and finely chopped
225g/8oz mushrooms, finely chopped
Salt
Ground white pepper
2.5ml/½ tsp chopped penny royal
5ml/1 tsp chopped parsley
5ml/1 tsp chopped dill
15ml/1 tbsp cornflour/cornstarch
140ml/¼ pint/½ cup natural yogurt
1 egg yolk

GARNISH
Chopped parsley

Put the butter, garlic and onion in a small bowl and cook on HIGH for 2 minutes until beginning to soften. Add the mushrooms and herbs, cover and cook on HIGH for 2-4 minutes until the mushrooms are

soft. Season with salt and pepper. Cut the plaice fillets in half, lengthwise, and spread the stuffing over the fillets. Roll up the fillets and place in a circle, seamed side down, in a shallow dish. Cover and cook on HIGH for 6 minutes or until the fish is cooked. Transfer to a serving dish and keep warm. Mix the cornflour/cornstarch with a little of the yogurt, add the remaining yogurt, egg yolk and any cooking liquor, season with salt and pepper, whisk and cook, uncovered, on HIGH for 1-2 minutes, whisking every 30 seconds until thickened slightly. Serve the fish rolls on a pool of sauce and sprinkle with chopped parsley.

Cheesy Fish Pie

PREPARATION TIME: 10 minutes

MICROWAVE COOKING TIME:
8-10 minutes

SERVES: 4 people

450g/1lb smoked haddock fillets
45ml/3 tbsps milk
15g/½ oz/1 tbsp butter
Salt
Freshly ground black pepper
15ml/1 tbsp chopped basil
15ml/1 tbsp chopped sage
120g/4oz mozzarella cheese, sliced
675g/1½ lbs potatoes, cooked and
   mashed with 30ml/2 tbsps milk and a
   pinch of nutmeg

Place the fish in an even layer in a shallow dish. Pour over the milk and dot with butter. Season to taste with salt and pepper. Sprinkle over the chopped herbs. Put the cheese slices on top of the fish and cover with the mashed potato. Cover and cook on HIGH for 8-10 minutes. Brown under the grill/broiler if desired.

Facing page: Smoky Haddock and Chive au Gratin (top) and Cheesy Fish Pie (bottom).

Trout with Lovage and Yogurt Sauce

PREPARATION TIME: 10 minutes

MICROWAVE COOKING TIME:
12-18 minutes

SERVES: 4 people

15ml/½ oz/1 tbsp butter
60g/2oz/½ cup flaked/slivered almonds
5ml/1 tsp celery seeds
30ml/2 tbsps chopped lovage
4 medium trout, cleaned
Salt
Freshly ground black pepper

15ml/1 tbsp cornflour/cornstarch
140ml/¼ pint/½ cup natural yogurt

Put the butter, almonds and celery seeds into a shallow dish and cook, uncovered, on HIGH for 4-8 minutes, stirring frequently, until the almonds begin to brown. Set aside. Divide about half the chopped lovage between the four trout, place inside each fish and season with salt and pepper. Arrange the fish head to tail in a shallow dish and cook on HIGH for 6-8 minutes until the fish is cooked, repositioning halfway through cooking. Set aside and keep

warm. Mix the cornflour/cornstarch with a little of the yogurt in a small bowl and then add the remaining yogurt. Cook on HIGH for 2-4 minutes, whisking frequently until thickened. Stir in remaining lovage. Serve the trout with the sauce and garnish with the browned almonds.

This page: Plaice with Herbed Mushrooms. Facing page: Trout with Lovage and Yogurt Sauce (top) and Orange Baked Fish (bottom).

Salmon Quiche

PREPARATION TIME: 10 minutes

MICROWAVE COOKING TIME:
14 minutes

SERVES: 4 people

120g/4oz/1 cup wholemeal/whole-
  wheat flour
Pinch of salt
60g/2oz/4 tbsps margarine
30-45ml/2-3 tbsps water
1 212g/7oz can of red salmon
150ml/5 fl. oz/⅔ cup natural yogurt
15ml/1 tbsp chopped dill
5ml/1 tsp lemon juice
10ml/2 tsps tomato purée/paste
5ml/1 tsp white wine vinegar
Salt
Pepper

GARNISH
Sprigs of dill

Put the flour and the salt in a mixing
bowl. Rub in the margarine until the
mixture resembles fine breadcrumbs.
Add enough water to mix to form a
wet dough. Put the pastry into a
16cm/6½ inch shallow flan dish and
press out to form a pie shell. Prick
the base with a fork and cook,
uncovered, on HIGH for 3-4
minutes. Turn every minute. Drain
the salmon and discard any bones
and skin. Place the salmon in a
mixing bowl with the yogurt, dill,
lemon juice, tomato purée/paste and
vinegar and mix well. Season to taste
and spread the mixture over the pie
shell. Cook, uncovered, on LOW for
10 minutes until hot. Garnish with
sprigs of dill.

Orange Baked Fish

PREPARATION TIME: 10 minutes

MICROWAVE COOKING TIME:
6-8 minutes

SERVES: 4 people

4 herrings
4 bay leaves
60g/2oz/4 tbsps butter

Juice and grated zest of ½ orange
15ml/1 tbsp chopped dill

GARNISH
Orange slices

Rinse the fish and dry well. Place a
bay leaf inside each fish. Place each
fish on a sheet of non-stick baking
parchment. Put the butter in a small
bowl and cook on HIGH for 15-30
seconds to soften slightly. Beat in the
orange juice, zest and dill. Divide the
butter into four and spread some
over each of the fish. Wrap each

**This page: Salmon Quiche. Facing
page: Mixed Vegetable Risotto
(top) and Paella (bottom).**

parcel separately, making sure the fish
is totally enclosed. Cook on HIGH
for 6-8 minutes, until the fish is
cooked, repositioning the fish
halfway through the cooking time.
Serve in the paper garnished with
orange slices.

VEGETABLES, PASTA & GRAINS

Paella

PREPARATION TIME: 10 minutes

MICROWAVE COOKING TIME: 20-25 minutes plus 5 minutes standing time

SERVES: 6 people

450g/1lb monkfish, cut into cubes
15ml/1 tbsp oil
1 small onion, peeled and finely sliced
1 clove garlic, peeled and crushed
225g/8oz/1 cup rice
570ml/1 pint/2 cups hot fish stock or water
Few saffron strands, soaked in 30ml/ 2 tbsps water (optional)
225g/8oz squid, cleaned and cut into rings
225g/8oz shelled mussels
120g/4oz shelled clams or cockles
30ml/2 tbsps chopped parsley
30ml/2 tbsps chopped coriander
Whole prawns/shrimp
Salt
Ground white pepper

Put the fish in a dish, cover and cook on HIGH for 4 minutes then set aside. Put the oil, onion and garlic in a large casserole and cook on HIGH for 2 minutes. Stir in the rice and cook on HIGH for 1 minute. Stir in the stock and saffron, if using. Add the squid and cook, uncovered, on HIGH for 10-15 minutes or until most of the liquid has been absorbed and the rice is almost cooked. Carefully stir in the shellfish, monkfish and herbs and cook on HIGH for 2 minutes. Cover and leave to stand for 5 minutes before serving. Serve garnished with the whole prawns/shrimp.

Mixed Vegetable Risotto

PREPARATION TIME: 15 minutes

MICROWAVE COOKING TIME:
25-30 minutes plus 5 minutes
standing time

SERVES: 4 people

15ml/1 tbsp oil
½ red pepper, seeded and diced
½ green pepper, seeded and diced
570ml/1 pint/2 cups hot vegetable stock
225g/8oz/1 cup brown rice
180g/6oz button mushrooms, quartered
10ml/2 tsps chopped pennyroyal
10ml/2 tsps chopped hyssop
Salt
Freshly ground black pepper
120g/4oz prawns/shrimp

Put the oil in a casserole and add the
diced peppers. Cover and cook on
HIGH for 3-4 minutes until the
peppers are beginning to soften. Add
the stock, rice, mushrooms, herbs
and seasoning. Stir, cover and cook
on HIGH for 25-30 minutes, or until
most of the liquid has been absorbed.
Stir in the prawns/shrimp and leave
to stand for 5 minutes before serving.

Cheese and Tomato Pasta

PREPARATION TIME: 10 minutes

MICROWAVE COOKING TIME:
17-23 minutes

SERVES: 4 people

15ml/1 tbsp oil
1 medium onion, peeled and finely
    chopped
120g/4oz mushrooms, finely sliced
15ml/1 tbsp tomato purée/paste
1 285g/10oz can tomatoes
30ml/2 tbsps fines herbes
90g/3oz strong Cheddar cheese, grated
15ml/1 tbsp Parmesan cheese
225g/8oz tagliatelle
850ml/1½ pints/3 cups boiling water

Put the oil in a medium bowl with
the onion and cook on HIGH for 2
minutes until softened. Add the
mushrooms, tomato purée/paste and
tomatoes and mix well, breaking up
the tomatoes slightly. Cook,
uncovered, on HIGH for 4-5 minutes
or until boiling. Cook for a further
3-4 minutes until reduced slightly.
Stir in the herbes, grated cheese and
Parmesan. Cover and keep warm. Put
the pasta and the water in a large
bowl. Cover and cook on HIGH for
8-10 minutes or until the pasta is
cooked. Drain and arrange on a
serving dish. Reheat the sauce on
HIGH for 1-2 minutes if necessary,
and pour over the pasta to serve.

Leek and Potato with Lemon Thyme

PREPARATION TIME: 10 minutes

MICROWAVE COOKING TIME:
8-10 minutes

SERVES: 4 people

225g/8oz leeks, trimmed, sliced and
    washed
225g/8oz potatoes, peeled and sliced
Salt
Freshly ground black pepper
30ml/2 tbsps chopped lemon thyme
140ml/¼ pint/½ cup hot vegetable stock

Arrange the leeks and potatoes in
layers in a micro-proof dish,
sprinkling each layer with salt, pepper
and lemon thyme. Pour over the
stock. Cover loosely and cook on
HIGH for 8-10 minutes until cooked.

Courgettes/Zucchini in Tomato-Bergamot Sauce

PREPARATION TIME: 10 minutes

MICROWAVE COOKING TIME:
10-15 minutes

SERVES: 4 people

700g/1½ lbs courgettes/zucchini
4 rashers streaky bacon, rinds removed,
    chopped
1 large onion, peeled and finely chopped
1 clove garlic, peeled and crushed
400g/14oz can tomatoes
30ml/2 tbsps bergamot
Salt
Freshly ground black pepper

Slice the courgettes/zucchini
diagonally and set aside. Put the
bacon into a small bowl and cook,
uncovered, on HIGH for 1-2 minutes
until crisp. Stir in the onion and
garlic and cook on HIGH for 2
minutes. Add the remaining
ingredients and mix well. Cover and
cook on HIGH for 10-15 minutes
until the vegetables are tender.

Nut and Herb Bulgur

PREPARATION TIME: 10 minutes

MICROWAVE COOKING TIME:
13 minutes plus 5 minutes
standing time

SERVES: 4-6 people

1 small red pepper, seeded and sliced
1 small onion, peeled and chopped
60g/2oz/½ cup hazelnuts, roughly
    chopped
30g/1oz/¼ cup pinenuts
15ml/1 tbsp oil
120g/4oz cucumber, diced
15ml/1 tbsp chopped coriander
15ml/1 tbsp chopped mint
30ml/2 tbsps chopped parsley
430ml/¾ pint/1½ cups hot chicken or
    vegetable stock
225g/8oz/1¼ cups bulgur wheat

Put the pepper, onions, nuts and oil
into a large bowl, cover and cook on
HIGH for 3 minutes. Stir in the
remaining ingredients. Cover and
cook on HIGH for 10 minutes or
until all the moisture has been
absorbed. Leave to stand for 5
minutes and fluff up with a fork
before serving. Serve hot or cold as
an alternative to rice.

**Facing page: Cheese and Tomato
Pasta (top) and Nut and Herb
Bulgur (bottom).**

Potato Cakes

PREPARATION TIME: 10 minutes

MICROWAVE COOKING TIME:
4 minutes

SERVES: 4 people

450g/1lb cooked potatoes
1 medium onion, peeled and finely
  chopped
30ml/2 tbsps fines herbes
5ml/1 tsp oil
Salt
Freshly ground black pepper

Mash the potato, add the onion and herbs; mix well. Divide the potato into four even portions and, using floured hands, form into four rounds about 2.5cm/1 inch thick. Preheat a large browning dish for the manufacturer's recommended time. Add the oil and quickly add the potato cakes, two at a time, and cook on HIGH for 2 minutes. Carefully turn over and cook on HIGH for a further 2 minutes until golden. Reheat the browning dish for a few minutes and repeat with the remaining potato cakes.

This page: Courgettes/Zucchini in Tomato-Bergamot Sauce. Facing page: Leek and Potato with Lemon Thyme (top) and Potato Cakes (bottom).

Rosemary Lyonnaise Potatoes

PREPARATION TIME: 10 minutes

MICROWAVE COOKING TIME: 12-15 minutes

SERVES: 4 people

450g/1lb potatoes
30g/1oz/2 tbsps butter
15ml/1 tbsp finely chopped rosemary
1 small clove garlic, peeled and crushed
1 small onion, peeled and finely chopped
30ml/2 tbsps milk
Salt
Pepper

Peel and thinly slice the potatoes. Put the butter, rosemary, garlic and onions in a 20cm/8 inch shallow dish and cook on HIGH for 3 minutes until soft. Stir in the milk, salt, pepper and potatoes and mix well. Spread out in the dish. Cover and cook on MEDIUM for 12-15 minutes until the potatoes are soft. Brown under a grill/broiler if desired.

Braised Fennel

PREPARATION TIME: 5 minutes

MICROWAVE COOKING TIME: 5-7 minutes

SERVES: 4-6 people

2 225g/8oz bulbs fennel, trimmed and shredded
10ml/2 tsps chopped lovage
60ml/4 tbsps hot vegetable or chicken stock
30ml/2 tbsps sherry
2.5ml/½ tsp celery seeds

Combine all the ingredients, except the celery seeds. Cover and cook on HIGH for 5-7 minutes until the fennel is just tender, stirring twice during cooking. Drain and transfer to a serving dish, sprinkle over the celery seeds and serve immediately.

Tarragon and Lemon Carrots

PREPARATION TIME: 5 minutes

MICROWAVE COOKING TIME: 10-12 minutes

SERVES: 4 people

450g/1lb carrots, peeled and finely sliced
15ml/1 tbsp lemon juice
90ml/6 tbsps water
2 sprigs of fresh tarragon

GARNISH
Chopped tarragon
Grated lemon zest

Put the carrots in a casserole with the lemon juice, water and tarragon. Cover and cook on HIGH for 10-12 minutes. Drain and discard the tarragon sprigs. Garnish with chopped tarragon and lemon zest.

This page: Tarragon and Lemon Carrots (top) and Braised Fennel (bottom). Facing page: Rosemary Lyonnaise Potatoes.

Vegetable Pasta Salad

PREPARATION TIME: 5 minutes

MICROWAVE COOKING TIME:
8-10 minutes

SERVES: 4 people

225g/8oz pasta bows
850ml/1½ pints/3 cups boiling water
1 210g/7oz can tuna
90g/3oz/⅔ cup sweetcorn kernels

90g/3oz/⅔ cup cooked, sliced green beans
4 spring/green onions, cut diagonally into ½ inch lengths
30ml/2 tbsps grated horseradish
15ml/1 tbsp lemon juice
60ml/4 tbsps mayonnaise
Salt
Freshly ground black pepper
15ml/1 tbsp chopped mint
15ml/1 tbsp chopped parsley

Put the pasta in a large bowl with the water. Cover and cook on HIGH for 8-10 minutes until tender. Drain and rinse with cold water, drain again and set aside. Break the tuna into large chunks, add the sweetcorn, green beans and onions, and mix well. Mix the horseradish with the lemon juice, mayonnaise and seasoning. Add to the pasta and toss to coat. Serve the pasta cold, sprinkled with the chopped mint and parsley.

Microwave
COOKING WITH HERBS

DESSERTS

Poached Pears with Raspberry Coulis

PREPARATION TIME: 15-20 minutes

MICROWAVE COOKING TIME:
6-11 minutes

SERVES: 4 people

140ml/¼ pint/½ cup water
30ml/2 tbsps honey
10ml/2 tsps lemon juice
Few sprigs hyssop
4 pears
225g/8oz fresh or frozen raspberries
*   (thawed if frozen)*
5ml/1 tsp chopped hyssop

GARNISH
Hyssop leaves

Put the water and honey in a large, shallow dish and cook, uncovered, for 1-2 minutes, stirring until the honey is dissolved. Add the lemon juice and hyssop sprigs. Peel the pears thinly and cut in half; carefully remove the core and stalk using a teaspoon. Place the pears in the syrup, cover and cook on HIGH for 5-10 minutes until the pears are tender. Meanwhile, purée the raspberries in a blender or food processor and then push the purée through a sieve to remove the pips. Sweeten the purée with a little of the cooking syrup if desired. Stir in the chopped hyssop. Carefully drain the pears and transfer to a serving dish. Chill thoroughly. Serve the pears

**Facing page: Vegetable Pasta Salad.
This page: Rhubarb Tansy (top)
and Poached Pears with Raspberry
Coulis (bottom).**

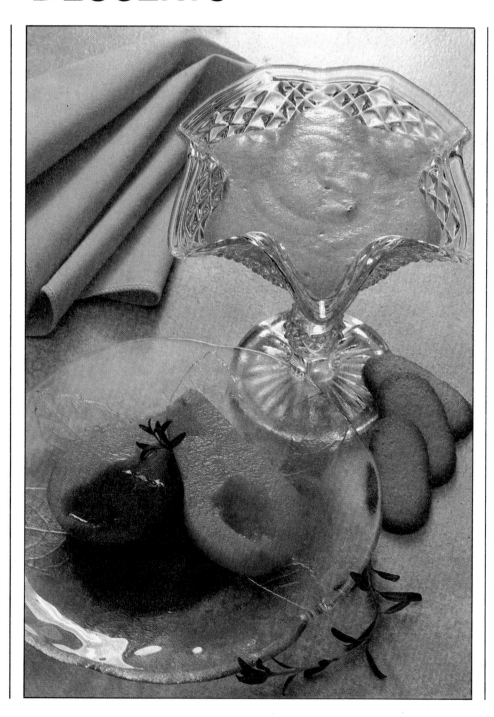

with a little of the raspberry coulis poured over them, serve the remaining coulis separately. Decorate with hyssop leaves if desired.

Rhubarb Tansy

PREPARATION TIME: 10 minutes

MICROWAVE COOKING TIME: 10-12 minutes

SERVES: 4 people

450g/1lb rhubarb, trimmed and cut into
  2.5cm/1 inch lengths
Pinch ground ginger
60ml/4 tbsps water
2 eggs, separated
Juice and zest of 1 lemon
90g/3oz/⅓ cup sugar
140ml/¼ pint/1½ cups double/heavy
  cream
10ml/2 tsps chopped tansy

Put the rhubarb in a large bowl with the ginger and water. Cover and cook on HIGH for 10-12 minutes, stirring twice, until the rhubarb is mushy. Stir in the egg yolk, tansy, lemon juice and zest. Purée in a food processor or blender. Whisk the egg-whites to soft peaks, then whisk in the sugar, half at a time. Whip the cream to soft peaks and fold into the rhubarb mixture; fold in the egg whites and spoon the mixture into glasses. Chill thoroughly before serving with crisp biscuits/cookies.

Grape and Bergamot Jellies

PREPARATION TIME: 10 minutes plus setting time

MICROWAVE COOKING TIME: 3-5 minutes

SERVES: 4 people

120g/4oz/green grapes
430ml/¾ pint/1½ cups unsweetened
  white grape juice
30g/2 tbsps sugar
15g/1 tbsp powdered gelatine
140ml/¼ pint/½ cup water
4 sprigs bergamot
Whipped cream to decorate (optional)

If the grapes are not seedless, cut in half and remove the pips. Skin the grapes if desired. Put the grape juice in a large bowl with the sugar and bergamot, and cook on HIGH for 2-4 minutes until the sugar is dissolved, stirring once. Allow to cool slightly, then remove the bergamot. Mix the gelatine with 60ml/4 tbsps/¼ cup of the water, cook on HIGH for 30 seconds, stir and cook for a further 30 seconds if necessary to dissolve the gelatine. Stir into the grape juice and add the remaining water. Divide the grapes between four glasses and pour in the jelly. Chill until set. Decorate with rosettes of cream if desired.

spearmint. Pour into the bottom of the pudding basin. Put the remaining ingredients except the applemint into a mixing bowl and beat thoroughly until smooth; fold in the applemint. Carefully spoon the mixture on top of the apple. Cook, uncovered, on HIGH for 6-7 minutes until the mixture is just dry on top and beginning to come away from the sides. Cover and leave to stand for 5 minutes before turning out onto a serving dish. Serve hot or cold with cream or ice cream.

Orange with Lemon Balm

PREPARATION TIME: 10 minutes plus chilling

MICROWAVE COOKING TIME: 7 minutes

SERVES: 4 people

4 oranges
140ml/¼ pint/½ cup sweet white wine
15-30ml/1-2 tbsps honey
15ml/1 tbsp Grand Marnier
15ml/1 tsp chopped lemon balm

GARNISH
Whole lemon balm leaves (optional)

Peel the oranges, removing all the white pith. Cut the oranges into slices and arrange on a serving dish. Mix the wine, honey to taste and Grand Marnier together in a small bowl, stir in the lemon balm and cook on HIGH for 2 minutes. Stir to dissolve the honey and cook on MEDIUM for 5 minutes or until slightly reduced and syrupy. Pour over the oranges and chill thoroughly. Garnish with whole lemon balm leaves if desired.

Applemint Pudding

PREPARATION TIME: 10 minutes

MICROWAVE COOKING TIME: 9-12 minutes plus 5 minutes standing time

SERVES: 4-6 people

225g/8oz cooking apple, peeled, cored and sliced
Small knob butter
30-60g/2-4 tbsps granulated sugar
5ml/1 tsp chopped spearmint
120g/4oz/½ cup margarine
120g/4oz/½ cup dark brown sugar
120g/4oz/1 cup plain/all-purpose flour
7.5ml/1½ tsps baking powder
2 eggs
10ml/2 tsps golden syrup
30ml/2 tbsps milk
10ml/2 tsps chopped applemint
Oil to grease

Lightly grease a 1150ml/2 pint/4 cup pudding basin or bowl. Place the apples, butter and sugar to taste in a small bowl, cover and cook on HIGH for 3-5 minutes until soft and mushy, stirring occasionally. Stir in the

Facing page: Grape and Bergamot Jellies (top) and Orange with Lemon Balm (bottom). This page: Applemint Pudding.

Microwave

COOKING WITH SPICES

SOUPS & STARTERS

Tomato Soup

PREPARATION TIME: 10 minutes

MICROWAVE COOKING TIME:
15-20 minutes

SERVES: 4 people

15ml/1 tbsp oil
2 carrots, peeled and finely chopped
1 onion, peeled and finely chopped
2.5ml/½ tsp ground allspice
1.25ml/¼ tsp ground ginger
2 rashers streaky bacon, rind removed and
  chopped
2 400g/14oz canned tomatoes
15ml/1 tbsp sugar
570ml/1 pint/2 cups hot vegetable or
  chicken stock
Salt
Freshly ground black pepper
30ml/2 tbsps cornflour/cornstarch
60ml/4 tbsps water
4 tomatoes, skinned and sliced

Put the oil, chopped vegetables,
spices and bacon in a large bowl.
Cover and cook on HIGH for 4-5
minutes. Add the canned tomatoes,
sugar and stock, cover and cook on
HIGH for 8-10 minutes or until
boiling. Reduce the setting to
MEDIUM and cook for 15 minutes.
Purée in a food processor or blender
if desired. Season to taste with salt
and pepper. Mix the cornflour/
cornstarch and water together and
add to the soup along with the sliced
tomatoes. Cook, uncovered, on
HIGH for 3-5 minutes, stirring once
until the soup is thickened slightly.

vegetables and cook on HIGH for 3 minutes. Pour in the stock, cover and cook on HIGH for 15-20 minutes until all the vegetables are tender. Purée in a food processor or blender. Return to the rinsed out bowl, season to taste with salt and pepper and cook on HIGH for 5 minutes until boiling. Stir in the cream and cook on HIGH for 1-2 minutes to heat through. Sprinkle with chopped parsley to serve.

Spicy Hot Grapefruit

PREPARATION TIME: 10 minutes

MICROWAVE COOKING TIME: 3-4 minutes

SERVES: 4 people

2 pink grapefruit
5ml/1 tsp allspice

GARNISH
Lemon balm

Cut the grapefruit in half. Using a sharp knife or grapefruit knife, cut around the edges of the fruit between the flesh and the pith. Then cut down between each segment, removing the skin from the flesh. Take the core between finger and thumb and pull out, removing the skin. Remove any pips. Sprinkle the allspice over each grapefruit half. Arrange in a circle in the microwave oven and cook on HIGH for 3-4 minutes until hot. Garnish with lemon balm leaves.

Country Cream Soup

PREPARATION TIME: 10 minutes

MICROWAVE COOKING TIME: 26-32 minutes

SERVES: 4 people

15ml/1 tbsp oil
1 large onion, peeled and chopped
5ml/1 tsp ground coriander
3 sticks celery, chopped
1-2 turnips, depending on size, peeled and chopped
3 carrots, peeled and chopped
850ml/1½ pints/3 cups good hot vegetable stock
Salt
Freshly ground black pepper
140ml/¼ pint/½ cup double/heavy cream

GARNISH
Chopped parsley

Put the oil, onion and coriander in a large bowl, cover and cook on HIGH for 2 minutes. Add the other

Facing page: Tomato Soup (top) and Country Cream Soup (bottom). This page: Spicy Hot Grapefruit.

Put the chicken livers and sherry together in a small bowl. Add the garlic and spices. Cover and cook on HIGH for 6-10 minutes, stirring twice. Place the mixture in a food processor and process until smooth. Add 225g/8oz of the butter and process again. Stir in the yogurt. Divide the mixture between 4 individual dishes or put in one large dish and chill slightly. Put the remaining butter in a jug and cook on HIGH for 1 minute or until bubbling. Leave to settle. Carefully pour a little of the clarified butter on top of the pâté, leaving behind the white sediment. Chill thoroughly before serving.

Sardine Spreading Pâté

PREPARATION TIME: 10 minutes plus chilling time

MICROWAVE COOKING TIME: 2½-4 minutes

SERVES: 8 people

2 120g/4oz cans sardines in oil
30g/1oz/2 tbsps flour
2.5ml/½ tsp ground cumin
2.5ml/½ tsp ground fenugreek
5ml/1 tsp ground mild chili powder
140ml/¼ pint/½ cup milk
Salt
Freshly ground black pepper
140ml/¼ pint/½ cup natural yogurt
15ml/1 tbsp lemon juice

Drain the sardines, reserving 30ml/ 2 tbsps of the oil. Put the oil in a bowl, stir in the flour and spices, and cook on HIGH for 45 seconds. Add the milk and season with salt and pepper. Cook on HIGH for 1-2 minutes, whisking frequently until the sauce is thickened. Mash the fish with a fork and stir into the sauce. Stir in the yogurt and lemon juice. Pour into individual ramekins/ custard cups or one large dish and chill thoroughly before serving. Garnish with parsley.

Spicy Chicken Liver Pâté

PREPARATION TIME: 15 minutes plus chilling time

MICROWAVE COOKING TIME: 7-11 minutes

SERVES: 8-10 people

450g/1lb chicken livers, roughly chopped

45ml/3 tbsps sherry
1 small clove of garlic, peeled and crushed
Pinch ground bay leaves
Pinch ground cloves
1.25ml/¼ tsp ground mace
Salt
Pepper
280g/10oz/1¼ cups butter
15ml/2 tbsps natural yogurt

MEAT & FISH DISHES

Pork with Spiced Apricot Sauce

PREPARATION TIME: 10 minutes

MICROWAVE COOKING TIME: 11-18 minutes

SERVES: 4 people

30ml/2 tbsps oil
1 small onion, peeled and chopped
1 small clove garlic, peeled and crushed
120g/4oz/1 cup ready-to-eat dried
   apricots, chopped
30ml/2 tbsps sherry
140ml/¼ pint/½ cup water
2.5ml/½ tsp five spice powder
4 boneless pork loin chops

Put 15ml/1 tbsp of the oil in a small bowl and add the onion and garlic. Cover and cook on HIGH for 6-8 minutes to soften. Add the apricots, sherry, water and five spice powder. Cover and cook on HIGH until soft and pulpy. Set aside and keep warm. Heat a browning dish for the manufacturer's recommended time, add the remaining oil and quickly press the chops down onto the surface of the dish, then turn over and press down again. Cook on HIGH for 5-10 minutes until the chops are cooked. The apricot sauce can be thinned with a little of the juice from the chops if desired. Serve the chops with the apricot sauce.

Facing page: Sardine Spreading Pâté (top) and Spicy Chicken Liver Pâté (bottom). This page: Pork with Spiced Apricot Sauce.

Chicken in White Wine

PREPARATION TIME: 10 minutes

MICROWAVE COOKING TIME:
26 minutes

SERVES: 4 people

1.3kg/3lb chicken
15ml/1 tbsp oil
1 large onion, peeled and sliced
5ml/1 tsp ground coriander
10ml/2 tsps fennel seeds
2.5ml/½ tsp mace
½ head celery
1 bulb fennel
60g/2oz/4 tbsps flour
430ml/¾ pint/1½ cups hot chicken stock
140ml/¼ pint/½ cup dry white wine
Salt
Freshly ground black pepper

Cut the chicken into eight pieces and remove the skin. Pre-seal the chicken in a browning dish or frying pan if desired. Put the oil and onion into a casserole with the spices. Cook, uncovered, on HIGH for 2 minutes. Cut the celery into 5cm/2 inch pieces, diagonally. Trim and shred the fennel. Add to the casserole and cook on HIGH for 4 minutes, stirring once. Stir in the flour, add the stock and wine and season to taste with salt and pepper. Add the chicken, cover and cook on HIGH for 20 minutes until the chicken is cooked and the vegetables are tender, stirring occasionally. If the chicken was pre-sealed, the final cooking time should be reduced by 5-10 minutes.

Sweet and Spicy Lamb

PREPARATION TIME: 10 minutes plus standing time

MICROWAVE COOKING TIME:
35 minutes

SERVES: 4 people

450g/1lb lamb fillet
1.25ml/¼ tsp ground ginger
1.25ml/¼ tsp ground cloves
1.25ml/¼ tsp ground mace

15ml/1 tbsp honey
15ml/1 tbsp Dijon mustard
1 clove garlic, peeled and crushed
30ml/2 tbsps white wine vinegar
1 red pepper, seeded and cut into 2.5cm/1 inch pieces
1 green pepper, seeded and cut into 2.5cm/1 inch pieces
6 spring/green onions, cut into 2.5cm/1 inch lengths
1 225g/8oz can pineapple cubes
120g/4oz mushrooms, quartered if large
140ml/¼ pint/½ cup hot chicken stock
15ml/1 tbsp cornflour/cornstarch
45ml/3 tbsps water

GARNISH
Spring/green onion brushes

Cut the lamb into 2.5cm/1 inch cubes. Combine the spices, honey, mustard, garlic and vinegar. Stir in the lamb and leave to marinate for 1-2 hours. Put the peppers and onions in a casserole and cook on HIGH for 2 minutes. Stir in the lamb, marinade, pineapple and juice, mushrooms and stock. Cover and cook on HIGH for 10 minutes then reduce setting and cook on MEDIUM for 20 minutes until the lamb is tender. Mix the cornflour/cornstarch and water and stir into the casserole. Cook, uncovered, on HIGH for 3-4 minutes, stirring once until the sauce is thickened. Garnish with spring/green onion brushes.

Pork with Spiced Pears

PREPARATION TIME: 10 minutes

MICROWAVE COOKING TIME:
20-25 minutes

SERVES: 4 people

4 225g/8oz pork chops
15ml/1 tbsp oil
1 medium onion, peeled and finely chopped
1 small clove garlic, peeled and crushed
Pinch ground cinnamon
Pinch ground cloves
Pinch ground cardamom
1.25ml/¼ tsp ground ginger

140ml/¼ pint/½ cup dry cider
2-3 firm pears, peeled, cored and sliced
15ml/1 tbsp cornflour/cornstarch
45ml/3 tbsps water
Salt
White pepper

Put the oil in a small dish, add the onions and garlic, and cook on HIGH for 2 minutes. Stir in the spices and cook on HIGH for 1 minute. Add the cider and the pears, mix well, cover and cook on HIGH for 8-10 minutes until the pears are soft, stirring occasionally. Mix the cornflour/cornstarch with the water and add to the pears. Cook on HIGH for 2 minutes, stirring once, until thickened. Season with salt and pepper and keep warm. Arrange the chops in a circle in a shallow dish, cover and cook on HIGH for 10 minutes or until cooked, turning over and re-arranging halfway through the cooking time. Arrange the chops on a serving dish and pour the sauce over. Cook on HIGH for 1-2 minutes to reheat the sauce, if necessary.

Saffron Chicken Avocados

PREPARATION TIME: 15 minutes

MICROWAVE COOKING TIME:
6-10 minutes

SERVES: 4 people

140ml/¼ pint/½ cup natural yogurt
Few strands saffron
2 chicken breast fillets, cut into slivers
10ml/2 tsps celery seeds
Salt
Ground white pepper

Facing page: Sweet and Spicy Lamb.

2 avocado pears
Lemon juice
2 sticks celery, chopped
60g/2oz/½ cup brown breadcrumbs
60g/2oz/½ cup grated Parmesan cheese

Mix the yogurt and saffron together and set aside. Put the chicken in a bowl with the celery seeds, salt and pepper. Cover and cook on HIGH for 3-5 minutes until the chicken is cooked, stirring once. Cut the

avocados in half and remove the stones. Scoop out the flesh, leaving 5mm/¼ inch lining inside the shell; sprinkle the scooped-out shell with lemon juice. Chop the flesh and add to the chicken. Stir in the celery and yogurt, and pile back into the shells. Mix the breadcrumbs and the cheese together and sprinkle over the top. Arrange in a circle in the microwave and cook, uncovered, on HIGH for 3-5 minutes until hot. Brown under a

grill/broiler if desired. To serve as a starter/appetizer, omit the breadcrumb topping and serve cold.

Spiced Stroganoff

PREPARATION TIME: 15 minutes

MICROWAVE COOKING TIME: 7-11 minutes

SERVES: 4 people

450g/1lb fillet steak
15ml/1 tbsp oil
1 large onion, peeled and sliced
1 small clove garlic, peeled and crushed
225g/8oz mushrooms, sliced
5ml/1 tsp brown mustard seeds
5ml/1 tsp ground cumin
5ml/1 tsp ground coriander
45ml/3 tbsps dry white wine
Salt
Pepper
140ml/¼ pint/½ cup sour cream
140ml/¼ pint/½ cup natural yogurt
    mixed with 10ml/2 tsps cornflour/
    cornstarch

Cut the meat into very thin strips and toss in the oil. Heat a large browning dish for the manufacturer's recommended time. Add the meat and stir. Add the onion and garlic and cook, uncovered, on HIGH for 2-4 minutes until the onions are soft and the meat is almost cooked. Stir in the mushrooms, spices, wine, salt and pepper, and cook, covered, on HIGH for 4-5 minutes. Stir in the cream, yogurt and cornflour, and cook, uncovered, on HIGH for 1-2 minutes to heat through, stirring once. Take care not to let the mixture boil once the cream is added. Serve on a bed of rice.

This page: Saffron Chicken Avocados. Facing page: Chicken in White Wine (top) and Pork with Spiced Pears (bottom).

Duck Breasts with Spicy Apple

PREPARATION TIME: 15 minutes

MICROWAVE COOKING TIME:
12-17 minutes

SERVES: 4 people

4 225g/8oz duck breast fillets
8 juniper berries, crushed
5ml/1 tsp ground cumin
2.5ml/½ tsp ground cardamom
30g/1oz/2 tbsps butter
1-2 green eating apples

Cut a slit horizontally in each of the duck breasts and set aside. Place the juniper berries, cumin, cardamom and butter in a small dish and cook, uncovered, on HIGH for 1-2 minutes, stirring once. Core the apples and cut into 5mm/¼ inch thick slices. Toss in the butter mixture and cook on HIGH for 1-2 minutes until the apples are just beginning to soften, but still hold their shape. Divide the apple slices between the duck and place into each slit. Arrange the duck breasts in a circle in a shallow dish. Cover and cook on HIGH for 10-15 minutes until the duck is cooked, turning and repositioning halfway through the cooking time if necessary. Serve with green vegetables or salad.

Goulash

PREPARATION TIME: 10 minutes

MICROWAVE COOKING TIME:
34-35 minutes

SERVES: 4 people

450g/1lb fillet steak, cut into 2.5cm/
*   1 inch cubes*
15ml/1 tbsp oil
2 large onions, peeled and sliced
2 carrots, peeled and sliced
1 clove garlic, peeled and crushed
10ml/2 tsps paprika
5ml/1 tsp caraway seeds
Pinch cayenne pepper

30g/2 tbsps flour
430ml/¾ pint/1½ cups hot beef stock
45ml/3 tbsps tomato purée/paste
45ml/3 tbsps natural yogurt

Heat a browning dish for the manufacturer's recommended time. Toss the meat in the oil and, when the dish is hot, quickly add the meat. Stir and cook on HIGH for 1 minute. Add the onions, carrots and the garlic. Cook on HIGH for 3-4 minutes until soft. Stir in the spices and the flour and cook on HIGH for 1 minute. Stir in the stock and tomato purée/paste. Cover and cook on HIGH for 10 minutes then reduce the setting and cook on LOW for 20 minutes or until the meat is tender. Stir in the yogurt just before serving.

This page: Duck Breasts with Spicy Apple. Facing page: Goulash (top) and Spiced Stroganoff (bottom).

Spiced Meat Loaf

PREPARATION TIME: 5 minutes

MICROWAVE COOKING TIME:
25-30 minutes plus 5 minutes
standing time

SERVES: 6-8 people

225g/8oz lean minced/ground lamb
225g/8oz lean minced/ground pork
120g/4oz/1 cup granary or wholemeal/
   whole-wheat breadcrumbs
1 egg
60g/2oz/½ cup desiccated coconut
4 tomatoes, skinned and chopped
60g/2oz/½ cup walnuts, chopped
2.5ml/½ tsp ground ginger
2.5ml/½ tsp ground cardamom
2.5ml/½ tsp ground coriander
Salt
Freshly ground black pepper
70ml/4½ tbsps milk

Put all the ingredients into a large
mixing bowl and blend thoroughly.
Put the mixture into a micro-proof
loaf dish. Cover loosely and cook on
MEDIUM for 25-30 minutes,
repositioning three times during
cooking. Leave to stand 5 minutes
before turning out. Serve hot or cold.

Cheese and Nut Burgers

PREPARATION TIME: 15 minutes

MICROWAVE COOKING TIME:
6 minutes plus 1 minute
standing time

SERVES: 4 people

225g/8oz minced/ground beef
225g/8oz minced/ground pork
Salt
Pepper
Pinch cayenne pepper
60g/2oz Red Leicester cheese
5ml/1 tsp caraway seeds
30g/1oz/¼ cup hazelnuts, chopped

Mix the beef and pork with the salt,
pepper and cayenne in a mixing bowl.
Shape into 8 flattened rounds, about
10cm/4 inches in diameter. Mix the
cheese, caraway seeds and nuts
together and place in the centre of
4 of the rounds. Top with the
remaining rounds and press the edges
together well to seal-in the filling.
Arrange in a circle on a dish lined
with absorbent kitchen paper and
cook on HIGH for 4 minutes. Turn
over and cook for a further 2
minutes. Leave to stand for 1 minute
before serving. Serve with a green
salad or in hamburger buns.
These burgers can be cooked in a
pre-heated browning dish, if desired,
for 4-5 minutes, turning once.

Cod and Prawn/Shrimp Bake

PREPARATION TIME: 10 minutes

MICROWAVE COOKING TIME:
9-13 minutes

SERVES: 4 people

450g/1lb cod
2 bay leaves
6 pink peppercorns
1 small piece fresh ginger, peeled and
   grated
2.5ml/½ tsp ground mace
70ml/4½ tbsps white wine
70ml/4½ tbsps fish stock or water
30g/1oz/2 tbsps butter
30g/1oz/2 tbsps flour
140ml/¼ pint/½ cup milk
180g/6oz prawns/shrimp
30g/1oz/½ cup salt and vinegar
   flavoured crisps/potato chips, crushed

Cut the cod into 2.5cm/1 inch
pieces and place in a shallow dish.
Add the bay leaves, peppercorns,
ginger, mace, wine and stock/water.
Cover and cook on HIGH for 4
minutes until the fish is almost
cooked. Cover and set aside. Put the
butter in a small bowl and cook on
HIGH for 30 seconds to melt. Add
the flour and cook on HIGH for 30
seconds. Add the fish cooking liquor
and the milk, and cook on HIGH for
2-4 minutes, whisking every minute
until thickened. Add the prawns/
shrimp, pour the sauce over the cod
and cook on HIGH for 2-4 minutes
until the sauce is hot and the fish is
fully cooked. Sprinkle with the
crushed crisps/chips.

Salade au Fruits de Mer

PREPARATION TIME: 10 minutes
plus chilling

MICROWAVE COOKING TIME:
6-10 minutes

SERVES: 6 people

8 scallops with roes attached
60ml/4 tbsps water
Squeeze lemon juice
180g/6oz monkfish, cubed
120g/4oz prawns/shrimp
120g/4oz mussels
120g/4oz scampi/langoustines

DRESSING
120g/4oz curd cheese
15-30ml/1-2 tbsps milk
70ml/4½ tbsps natural yogurt
Salt
Ground white pepper
·Juice of ½ lemon
5ml/1 tsp Dijon mustard
5ml/1 tsp chili powder
Pinch cayenne pepper

Cut the scallops in half, horizontally,
and place with the monkfish, water
and lemon juice in a large bowl.
Cover and cook on MEDIUM for
5-8 minutes. Stir in the remaining
shellfish and cook on HIGH for 1-2
minutes. Leave to cool in the liquid,
then drain well. Blend the cheese,
milk and yogurt together in a food
processor or blender, add the lemon
juice, salt and pepper, and stir in the
mustard and spices. Toss the seafood
in the dressing to serve.

**Facing page: Cheese and Nut
Burgers (top) and Spiced Meat Loaf
(bottom).**

Creamy Prawn/Shrimp Flan

PREPARATION TIME: 15 minutes

MICROWAVE COOKING TIME: 9-12 minutes

SERVES: 4 people

120g/4oz/1 cup wholemeal/whole-
  wheat flour
Salt
60g/2oz/4 tbsps margarine
30-45ml/2-3 tbsps water
30g/1oz/2 tbsps butter
30g/1oz/2 tbsps flour
140ml/¼ pint/½ cup milk
30ml/2 tbsps dry white wine
90g/6 tbsps full fat cream cheese
225g/8oz prawns/shrimp
2.5ml/½ tsp paprika
Pinch cayenne pepper
2.5ml/½ tsp curry powder
Freshly ground black pepper
30ml/2 tbsps Parmesan cheese

GARNISH
Chopped parsley

Put the flour, salt and margarine into
a mixing bowl and rub in the fat until
the mixture resembles fine
breadcrumbs. Gradually add the
water and mix to form a soft dough.
Roll out the pastry and line a 20cm/
8 inch flan dish. Prick the base with a
fork and cook, uncovered, on HIGH
for 2-4 mins, turning during cooking.
Put the butter in a small bowl and
cook on HIGH for 45 seconds to
melt. Add the flour, mix well and
cook on HIGH for a further
1 minute. Add the milk, wine and
cream cheese. Whisk, then cook on
HIGH for 2-3 minutes until
thickened, whisking occasionally.
Add the remaining ingredients and
mix well. Pour into the pastry case.
Chill through to serve cold, or serve
hot by cooking, uncovered, on HIGH
for 3-4 minutes. Sprinkle with
chopped parsley.

**This page: Salade au Fruits de Mer.
Facing page: Creamy Prawn/
Shrimp Flan (top) and Cod and
Prawn/Shrimp Bake (bottom).**

Red Mullet en Papillote

PREPARATION TIME: 10 minutes

MICROWAVE COOKING TIME: 9-11 minutes

SERVES: 4 people

2 carrots, peeled and cut into matchsticks
Salt
45ml/3 tbsps water
60g/2oz/¼ cup water chestnuts, cut into
  sticks
60g/2oz/1 cup bean sprouts
Small piece lemon grass, peeled and
  chopped or 5ml/1 tsp grated lemon zest
10ml/2 tsps aniseed
5ml/1 tsp dill seeds
60ml/4 tbsps white wine
4 red mullet, cleaned
15g/1 tbsp butter
Ground white pepper

Put the carrots, salt and water in a
bowl and cook on HIGH for 2
minutes. Add the water chestnuts
and cook on HIGH for 1 minute. Stir
in the bean sprouts, lemon grass or
lemon zest, aniseed, dill seeds and
wine. Place each fish on a piece of
non-stick baking parchment or wax
paper. Divide the vegetables between

the four fish and pour over the liquid. Season with pepper, dot with the butter and wrap each parcel separately, ensuring that each fish is totally enclosed. Place in the microwave and cook on HIGH for 6-8 minutes until the fish is cooked, repositioning halfway through cooking time. Serve the fish in their parcels.

Mackerel with Ginger and Lime

PREPARATION TIME: 5 minutes

MICROWAVE COOKING TIME: 6-8 minutes

SERVES: 4 people

4 small mackerel, cleaned and trimmed
140ml/¼ pint/½ cup fish stock or water
10ml/2 tsps freshly grated ginger
Juice and grated zest of 1 lime

GARNISH
Lime slices
Parsley

Arrange the mackerel head to tail in a shallow dish. Mix the remaining ingredients together and pour over the fish. Cover and cook on HIGH for 6-8 minutes or until the fish is cooked. Carefully transfer the fish to a serving dish and serve garnished with lime slices and parsley.

Curried Fish

PREPARATION TIME: 15 minutes

MICROWAVE COOKING TIME: 11-15 minutes

SERVES: 4 people

450g/1lb monkfish
15ml/1 tbsp oil
15ml/1 tbsp curry powder
10ml/2 tsps garam masala
2.5ml/½ tsp ground ginger
6 spring/green onions, sliced
1-2 small turnips, peeled and diced
4 tomatoes, skinned and chopped
225g/8oz sweet potato, peeled and cubed
140ml/¼ pint/½ cup natural yogurt
60g/2oz/½ cup cashew nuts

Cut the fish into 2.5cm/1 inch cubes and set aside. Put the oil and the spices in a casserole and cook on HIGH for 1 minute. Stir in the onions, turnip, tomatoes and sweet potatoes. Cover and cook on HIGH for 5-7 minutes until just tender. Add the fish and continue cooking on HIGH for 5-6 minutes until the fish and vegetables are cooked. Stir in the yogurt and cashews, cook on HIGH for 1-2 minutes until heated through, stirring once.

This page: Curried Fish. Facing page: Mackerel with Ginger and Lime (top) and Red Mullet en Papillote (bottom).

VEGETABLES, PASTA & GRAINS

Carrots with Cumin

PREPARATION TIME: 5 minutes

MICROWAVE COOKING TIME: 10-12 minutes

SERVES: 4 people

450g/1lb carrots, peeled
70ml/4½ tbsps hot vegetable stock or
    water
10ml/2 tsps cumin
Salt
Freshly ground black pepper
15g/½ oz/1 tbsp butter
10ml/2 tsps chopped parsley

Cut the carrots into thin strips about 5-7cm/2-3 inches long, and place them in a casserole with the vegetable stock, cumin, salt and pepper. Cover and cook on HIGH for 10-12 minutes, stirring once. Stir in the butter and toss well. Serve sprinkled with parsley.

Festive Brussels Sprouts

PREPARATION TIME: 5 minutes

MICROWAVE COOKING TIME: 10 minutes

SERVES: 4 people

450g/1lb Brussels sprouts
225g/8oz/1¼ cups fresh chestnuts,
    roughly chopped
60ml/4 tbsps water
Salt
30g/1oz/2 tbsps butter
2.5ml/½ tsp aniseed
Freshly ground black pepper

Remove outer leaves from the

sprouts, if necessary, and cut a cross in the bottom of each. Put the chestnuts in a casserole with the water and salt. Cover and cook on HIGH for 2 minutes. Add the sprouts, cover and cook for 7-8 minutes until tender, stirring once. Drain well. Put the butter in a small bowl and cook on HIGH for 30 seconds until melted. Stir in the aniseed and pepper. Pour the melted butter over the sprouts and toss to serve.

This page: Green Beans with Mustard Sauce. Facing page: Festive Brussels Sprouts (top) and Carrots with Cumin (bottom).

NB: To remove the chestnut shells, cut a slit in the base of each chestnut and cook, a few at a time, on HIGH for 2-3 minutes then remove shells.

Cabbage with Caraway

PREPARATION TIME: 5 minutes

MICROWAVE COOKING TIME:
7 minutes

SERVES: 4 people

450g/1lb green cabbage
60ml/4 tbsps water
Salt
30g/1oz/2 tbsps butter
30ml/2 tbsps caraway seeds
Freshly ground black pepper

Finely shred the cabbage and place in a roasting bag with the salt and water. Tie loosely and cook on HIGH for 5-6 minutes until cooked but still slightly crisp. Drain well. Place the butter in a large bowl and cook on HIGH for 1 minute or until melted. Add the caraway seeds and pepper and stir well. Add the cooked cabbage and toss. Serve garnished with extra caraway seeds if desired.

Green Beans with Mustard Sauce

PREPARATION TIME: 15 minutes

MICROWAVE COOKING TIME:
9-12 minutes

SERVES: 4 people

450g/1lb green beans
140ml/¼ pint/½ cup hot vegetable stock
*   or water*
Salt
Approx. 140ml/¼ pint/½ cup milk
30g/1oz/2 tbsps butter
30g/1oz/2 tbsps flour
15ml/1 tbsp dry mustard
Ground white pepper

Trim the green beans and cut into 5cm/2 inch lengths. Put the beans in

Gingered Swede

PREPARATION TIME: 10 minutes

MICROWAVE COOKING TIME:
11-17 minutes

SERVES: 4 people

450g/1lb swede, peeled
60ml/4 tbsps water
Salt
Freshly ground white pepper
15g/½oz/1 tbsp butter
30ml/2 tbsps fresh ginger, peeled and
*   grated*

GARNISH
Fresh ginger, peeled and cut into thin strips

Cut the swede into small pieces and place in a bowl with the water, salt and pepper. Loosely cover and cook on HIGH for 10-15 minutes or until tender, stirring twice. Drain well and mash thoroughly or purée in a food processor with the butter. Stir in the ginger. Reheat on HIGH for 1-2 minutes if necessary. Serve hot. Garnish with fresh ginger if desired.

This page: Spiced Couscous with Chicken and Prawns/Shrimp. Facing page: Cabbage with Caraway (top) and Gingered Swede (bottom).

a casserole with the vegetable stock or water and salt. Cover and cook on HIGH for 6-8 minutes until just tender, stirring once. Drain, reserving the cooking liquor. Set the beans aside and keep warm. Make the liquor up to 280ml/½ pint/1 cup with the milk. Put the butter into a bowl and cook on HIGH for 30 seconds or until melted. Add the flour, mustard powder and pepper and mix well. Cook on HIGH for 45 seconds. Add the milk and cooking liquor and mix well. Cook, uncovered, on HIGH for 1 minute. Cook a further 1-2 minutes until thickened slightly, whisking every 30 seconds. Serve the sauce poured over the beans.

Spiced Couscous with Chicken and Prawns/ Shrimp

PREPARATION TIME: 5 minutes

MICROWAVE COOKING TIME: 9-14 minutes

SERVES: 4 people

225g/8oz/1½ cups couscous
430ml/¾ pint/1½ cups water
Pinch salt
15ml/1 tbsp oil
10ml/2 tsps ground coriander
10ml/2 tsps ground fenugreek
5ml/1 tsp ground cardamom
2 chicken breast fillets, cubed
3 spring/green onions, sliced diagonally
120g/4oz prawns/shrimp

GARNISH
Whole prawns/shrimp

Put the couscous, water and salt into a large bowl and leave to stand while cooking the chicken. Put the oil and spices into a bowl and cook, uncovered, on HIGH for 1 minute. Toss the chicken in the oil and spice mixture, cover and cook on HIGH for 3-5 minutes until the chicken is cooked. Add the chicken and onions to the couscous (which will have absorbed much of the water) and mix well. Cover and cook on HIGH for

5-8 minutes, stirring in the prawns/ shrimp after 3 minutes. Fluff up with a fork before serving. Garnish with whole prawns/shrimp.

Lasagne Blanc

PREPARATION TIME: 10 minutes

MICROWAVE COOKING TIME: 30-40 minutes

SERVES: 4 people

1 onion peeled and studded with 6 cloves
1 bay leaf
Pinch nutmeg
5ml/1 tsp mustard seeds
430ml/¾ pint/1½ cups milk
120g/4oz mushrooms, sliced
70ml/4½ tbsps white wine
45g/1½ oz/3 tbsps butter
45g/1½ oz/3 tbsps flour
Salt
Ground white pepper
225g/8oz gammon/ham, diced
120g/4oz/¾ cup peas
60ml/4 tbsps double/heavy cream
180g/6oz ready-to-use dried lasagne noodles
120g/4oz/1 cup Cheddar cheese, grated

Put the onion, bayleaf, nutmeg and mustard seeds in the milk, cover and cook on HIGH for 3-5 minutes until just boiling. Leave to stand for 10 minutes. Meanwhile, put the mushrooms in a small bowl with the wine, cover and cook on HIGH for 4-5 minutes until soft. Put the butter in a bowl and cook on HIGH for 30 seconds-1 minute until melted. Stir in the flour and cook on HIGH for 45 seconds. Strain the milk and add with the wine. Whisk well. Cook, uncovered, on HIGH for 3-4 minutes until the sauce begins to thicken, whisking frequently. Season with salt and pepper, stir in the gammon/ham, peas, cooked mushrooms, and the cream. Arrange layers of sauce and lasagne in a microproof serving dish. Sprinkle the top with cheese and cook on MEDIUM for 20-25 minutes until the lasagne is fully cooked and the dish is heated through. Brown under the grill/ broiler if desired.

Spaghetti alla Bolognese

PREPARATION TIME: 10 minutes

MICROWAVE COOKING TIME: 40-50 minutes

SERVES: 4 people

225g/8oz spaghetti
1 clove garlic, peeled and crushed
1 large onion, peeled and finely chopped
1 stick celery, finely chopped
2.5ml/½ tsp ground allspice
1.25ml/¼ tsp ground cardamom
225g/8oz minced/ground beef
1 400g/14oz can tomatoes
Worcestershire sauce
70ml/4½ tbsps beef stock
Freshly ground black pepper
Salt
15ml/1 tbsp cornflour/cornstarch
45ml/3 tbsps sherry
1150ml/2 pints/4 cups boiling, salted water
15ml/1 tbsp oil
Grated Parmesan cheese to serve

Put the oil, garlic, onion, celery, and spices in a large bowl. Cover and cook on HIGH for 3-4 minutes until soft. Add the meat and cook on HIGH for 5-6 minutes until it has changed colour, breaking up with a fork once or twice during cooking. Add the tomatoes, Worcestershire sauce and stock, and season to taste with the salt and pepper. Cover and cook on LOW for 20 minutes until the meat is tender and the flavours well blended. Mix the cornflour/ cornstarch and sherry together and stir into the sauce. Cook on HIGH for 2-3 minutes until thickened slightly, stirring once. Cover, set aside and keep warm. Put the spaghetti and water in a large bowl, cover and cook on HIGH for 8-10 minutes. Drain and mix with the sauce. Reheat for 1-2 minutes if necessary. Sprinkle with Parmesan cheese to serve.

Facing page: Lasagne Blanc (top) and Spaghetti alla Bolognese (bottom).

73

Red Hot Slaw

PREPARATION TIME: 10 minutes

MICROWAVE COOKING TIME:
4 minutes

SERVES: 8 people

450g/1lb red cabbage, shredded
2 red onions, peeled and finely sliced
1 small white radish, peeled and grated
60ml/4 tbsps mayonnaise
60ml/4 tbsps natural yogurt
10ml/2 tsps grated horseradish
2.5ml/½ tsp aniseed
2.5ml/½ tsp chili powder

Mix the cabbage, onion and radish
together in a large bowl. Cook,
uncovered, on HIGH for 4 minutes
until the vegetables are hot, but not
beginning to cook. Mix together the
mayonnaise, yogurt, horseradish,
aniseed and chili powder and stir
into the hot vegetables.

Wild Rice Pilau

PREPARATION TIME: 5 minutes

MICROWAVE COOKING TIME:
14-17 minutes plus 5 minutes
standing time

SERVES: 4 people

15ml/1 tbsp oil
Piece cassia bark
4 black cardamom pods, crushed
8 cloves
4 black peppercorns
Piece star anise
180g/6oz/⅔ cup long grain rice
60g/2oz/¼ cup wild rice
570ml/1 pint/2 cups hot vegetable stock
60ml/4 tbsps dry white wine
60g/2oz/¼ cup flaked almonds
60g/2oz/¼ cup raisins

Put the oil and the spices in a
casserole and cook on HIGH for
1 minute. Stir in the rice and cook on
HIGH for a further 1 minute. Add
the stock, wine, nuts and raisins.
Cook, uncovered, on HIGH for 12-15
minutes or until most of the liquid
has been absorbed. Stir the rice and
quickly cover with a lid and leave to
stand for 5 minutes before serving.

Spicy Egg Fried Rice

PREPARATION TIME: 5 minutes

MICROWAVE COOKING TIME:
5-9 minutes

SERVES: 4 people

15ml/1 tbsp oil
1 small green chili, seeded and finely
*   chopped (optional)*
Small piece root ginger, peeled and grated
340g/12oz/4½ cups cooked rice
30ml/2 tbsps light soy sauce
2 eggs
2.5ml/½ tsp five spice powder

Put the oil, chili and ginger in a
medium bowl and cook on HIGH for
1-2 minutes until soft. Add the rice
and cook, uncovered, on HIGH for
2-4 minutes until the rice is hot. In a
small dish, beat the soy sauce with
the eggs and five spice powder, then
add to the rice. Cook, uncovered, on
HIGH for 2-3 minutes, stirring
regularly until the egg is cooked.

**This page: Red Hot Slaw. Facing
page: Wild Rice Pilau (top) and
Spicy Egg Fried Rice (bottom).**

Microwave
COOKING WITH SPICES

DESSERTS & CAKES

Orange Cinnamon Pudding

PREPARATION TIME: 5 minutes

MICROWAVE COOKING TIME:
16-20 minutes

SERVES: 4 people

120g/4oz/1 cup small pasta rings or other
  small soup pasta
430ml/¾ pint/1½ cups boiling water
60g/2oz/½ cup sultanas/golden raisins
30ml/2 tbsps golden syrup
Grated zest of 1 orange
410g/14½ oz can evaporated milk
2.5ml/½ tsp ground cinnamon

Put the pasta and water in a large
bowl which is big enough to allow for
boiling (about 1½ litres/3 pints/6
cups), cover and cook on HIGH for
8-10 minutes until the pasta is tender.
Stir in the remaining ingredients,
reserving a little zest for decorating.
Cook, uncovered, on HIGH for 8-10
minutes, stirring occasionally until it
is hot and creamy. Serve decorated
with orange zest.

Spiced Fruit Compôte

PREPARATION TIME: 10 minutes

MICROWAVE COOKING TIME:
10-12 minutes

SERVES: 4 people

280ml/½ pint/1 cup apple juice
280ml/½ pint/1 cup water
15-30ml/1-2 tbsps honey
Pinch cloves
Pinch nutmeg
1.25ml/¼ tsp aniseed

450g/1lb dried fruit salad
1 orange, peeled and segmented
4 fresh dates, stoned and halved
30ml/2 tbsps Cointreau

Combine the apple juice, water,
honey and spices in a large bowl.
Add the dried fruit, cover and cook
on HIGH for 10-12 minutes until the

fruit is just tender. Stir in the orange
segments, dates and Cointreau. Chill
thoroughly before serving.

**This page: Spiced Fruit Compôte.
Facing page: Chocolate and Coffee
Mousse (top) and Orange
Cinnamon Pudding (bottom).**

Chocolate and Coffee Mousse

PREPARATION TIME: 10 minutes

MICROWAVE COOKING TIME: 4 minutes

SERVES: 4 people

280ml/½ pint/1 cup milk
4 cardamom pods, crushed
Small piece of cinnamon stick
1.25ml/¼ tsp ground nutmeg
2 eggs, separated
60g/2oz/¼ cup caster sugar
30g/2 tbsps cornflour/cornstarch
60g/2oz plain/semi-sweet chocolate, grated
5ml/1 tsp coffee dissolved in 15ml/1 tbsp boiling water

GARNISH
Whipped cream
Grated chocolate

Put the milk in a jug with the cardamom, cinnamon and nutmeg. Cook on HIGH for 1-2 minutes until almost boiling. Cream together the egg yolks and sugar in a large bowl until light and fluffy. Stir in the cornflour/cornstarch. Strain the milk and gradually blend into the mixture. Stir in the chocolate. Cook on HIGH for 1½-2 minutes, stirring frequently until boiling and beginning to thicken. Stir in the coffee. Whisk the egg whites to soft peaks and fold into the chocolate mixture. Pour into individual dishes and chill until firm. Decorate with cream and chocolate.

Ginger Biscuits/Cookies

PREPARATION TIME: 10 minutes

MICROWAVE COOKING TIME: 8-12 minutes plus standing time

MAKES: approx. 24

120g/4oz/½ cup butter or soft margarine
60g/2oz/¼ cup dark brown sugar
15ml/1 tbsp black treacle/molasses
Small piece of ginger, peeled and grated
15ml/1 tbsp sesame seeds

180g/6oz/1½ cups plain/all-purpose flour
Pinch salt

Place the butter and sugar in a mixing bowl and cream together until light and fluffy. Beat in the treacle/molasses. Stir in the ginger and sesame seeds. Sift the flour and salt together into the bowl and mix to form a soft dough, adding a few teaspoons of water if necessary. Roll the dough into approximately 24 balls. Arrange 6 at a time in a circle on a sheet of non-stick baking parchment and place in the microwave. Flatten slightly and cook on HIGH for 2-2½ minutes. Allow to stand for a few minutes before transferring them to a wire rack to cool completely. Repeat with the remaining mixture.

This page: Spicy Carrot Cake (top) and Ginger Biscuits/Cookies (bottom). Facing page: Mincemeat and Apple Flan.

Mincemeat and Apple Flan

PREPARATION TIME: 20 minutes

MICROWAVE COOKING TIME: 6-7 minutes

SERVES: 6 people

120g/4oz/1 cup wholemeal/whole-wheat flour
Salt
60g/2oz/¼ cup margarine
60g/4 tbsps dark brown sugar
30-45ml/2-3 tbsps water
225g/8oz/1 cup sweet mincemeat
5ml/1 tsp ground nutmeg

1-2 green dessert apples, sliced
5ml/1 tsp ground allspice
15ml/1 tbsp brandy

Put the flour, salt and margarine into a mixing bowl and rub in the fat until the mixture resembles fine breadcrumbs. Stir in the sugar and gradually add the water, mixing to form a wet dough. Put the pastry into a 16cm/6½ inch flan dish and press out to form a pie shell. Prick the base of the shell with a fork and cook, uncovered, on HIGH for 3-4 minutes, turning the dish 3 times during cooking. Mix the mincemeat with the nutmeg, mix in the brandy and spread over the pastry base. Arrange the apple slices on top. Sprinkle the allspice over the apple. Cook, uncovered, on HIGH for 3 minutes until the flan is hot and the apples are just tender.

Spicy Carrot Cake

PREPARATION TIME: 10 minutes

MICROWAVE COOKING TIME: 8-10 minutes

SERVES: 6-8 people

120g/4oz/½ cup dark brown sugar
120g/4oz/½ cup margarine
2 eggs
15ml/1 tbsp mixed spice
60g/2oz/½ cup plain/all-purpose flour
60g/2oz/½ cup granary flour
2.5ml/½ tsp baking powder
45ml/3 tbsps milk
120g/4oz/¾ cup carrots, peeled and finely grated
225g/8oz low fat cheese
30ml/2 tbsps clear honey
2.5ml/½ tsp cinnamon
Walnut halves to decorate

Put the sugar and the margarine together in a bowl and cream with an electric mixer until light and fluffy. Add the eggs one at a time, beating well after each addition. Sift the mixed spice, plain/all-purpose flour and baking powder together and fold into the creamed mixture. Fold in the granary flour, milk and carrots. Place the mixture in a greased, 16cm/6 inch deep cake dish or soufflé dish. Cook, uncovered, on HIGH for 8-10 minutes. The dish should be turned 3 times during cooking. Leave to stand 5 minutes before turning out to cool on a wire rack. Beat the cheese, honey and cinnamon together in a bowl and spread the mixture over the top and sides of the cake. Decorate with walnut halves.

Microwave

HERBS & SPICES

INDEX